KAT THE DOG

Alyson Sheldrake is the author of the *Algarve Dream* series, and the author/curator of the *Travel Stories* series of anthologies. She lives in the Algarve, Portugal.

"The most uplifting animal memoir since *A Street Cat Named Bob*."

"This is the kind of read that causes hearts to ache, spirits to soar, and souls to sing with joy.

Against the odds, Kat battles for survival in a world that seems devoid of kindness, with only hope to cling to as she embarks on a perilous quest for a place to call home. With the open road finally behind her, Kat faces an even greater challenge – will she ever be able to shake off her deep-seated fear and uncertainty to embrace a new life founded on trust?

Alyson Sheldrake combines empathy and imagination to deliver a unique insight into the canine psyche. The result is an enchanting narrative which leaves the reader spellbound from beginning to end.

So much more than just another animal story, Kat the Dog is a tale of courage, compassion and, above all, unshakeable and unconditional love."

Liza Grantham, author of the Mad Cow in Galicia memoir series.

"Kat the Dog is a perfect meld of imagination and memoir. It relates the story of a young dog's journey from sad neglect to happiness in an uplifting tale of rescue and love. Alyson Sheldrake has depicted Kat's character beautifully and has written **a delightful, warm-hearted, gentle book that will touch any reader's heart**, but especially those who love dogs."

Valerie Poore, author of the Watery Ways and African Ways series of memoirs.

"Such a beautiful book, a memoir written from a dog's point of view. **It's beautiful, sad, emotional, and heartstring-tugging.** A story that will make you well up - but also weep with joy later. The book fills in what happened leading up to Kat's new life in Portugal. It's very special, a lovely story, and a wonderful ending for Alyson, Dave and Kat. Magical."

Julie Haigh, Amazon Reviewer.

"Triumph over adversity. **A gripping tale for animal lovers that will capture hearts and imaginations.** I couldn't put it down."

Beth Haslam, author of the Fat Dogs and French Estates series.

"***Black Beauty* for dog lovers.**"

"A remarkable book which made me sob and made me jump for joy. But most of all, it made me want to give this courageous little dog a huge hug."

Lisa Rose Wright, author of the Writing Home series of travelogue memoirs.

Kat
THE DOG

The remarkable tale of a rescued
Spanish water dog

ALYSON
SHELDRAKE

Copyright © 2022 Alyson Sheldrake

Cover designed by MiblArt

Website: www.miblart.com

Front cover photograph of Kat the Dog © Dave Sheldrake Photography

Formatted by Publish with Ant Press

Website: www.antpress.org

Published by Tadornini Publishing, 2022

First Edition

Kat the Dog – The remarkable tale of a rescued Spanish water dog

Paperback ISBN: 9789893331149

Hardback ISBN: 9789893331583

*This book is dedicated to everyone that has
known the love of a rescued animal.*

PROLOGUE

"Mommy, look over there at that doggie. She looks like a sheep."

The little boy pointed at the dog walking past them on the other side of the road. She had black curly fur, a stocky body, and a determined face. Her eyes were the colour of milk chocolate, deep and expressive, although half-hidden under the profusion of curls cascading over her face. A splash of white fur around her muzzle trickled down her throat onto her chest, making her seem older than her years.

She placed her paws delicately on the ground as she pranced along, elegant and assured, like a Lipizzaner on parade. She knew the boy was talking about her, as she lifted her head a little higher and wagged her tail.

"Why has she got such a short stump for a tail?" the boy asked his mother. "Surely all dogs have long tails?"

"Some dogs are born with very short tails, others none at all. And sometimes nasty people cut off their tails when they're still young pups."

The dog stopped to see what was happening.

"She's a pretty girl, isn't she? I think she knows we're talking about her."

I do indeed; the dog thought to herself.

"Is that what this book's all about, then?" asked the boy. "Her remarkable tail?"

"Not quite. This is a remarkable t-a-l-e. It's the story of that special little dog over there. And she has quite a story to tell…"

CHAPTER ONE

My mother, Rosa, gave birth to me alone. The wind slunk under the creaking wooden doors of the barn, whipping the straw around her as she huddled up and tried to keep warm. At least the farmer had dragged her inside as the first spasms of labour hit her frail old body.

The cows shuffled their hooves behind her; the sound clattering on the cold concrete floor. They were restless, as if they knew something was about to happen. It had been several days since the farmer had cleaned out the shed, and the stench of the cows' excrement was sickening. Rosa whimpered as a sharp pain clawed inside her, and then her pups were born, sliding silently out of her body. Rosa tended them, licking the slimy sacs and chewing each cord to release their bodies. Her body shuddered as the wind circled the floor and scattered dust across her bed.

She counted five pups as she drifted in and out of consciousness, barely noticing that none of them were moving. I was her sixth and final pup, and I slipped out, slithering onto the cold concrete. My mother gnawed at my cord, then fell asleep exhausted. She did not even realise I was alive.

I wriggled out from under the other pups and crawled to her belly, grasping at a teat as I grappled my way through the tangle of bodies.

The next morning, the barn door swung open, and the farmer strode over to where my mother lay sleeping beside me and the other pups. Rosa opened her eyes as he loomed overhead and instinctively curled her body around us. The farmer's rough hand grazed her belly as he lifted each pup in turn and spun them in the air.

"Useless," he cried, as he tossed each one into a plastic sack. "All dead."

He picked me up last, and I let out a faint squeak. The farmer stopped and held his arms out, stared at me, then spoke to my mother. "So, you have given me one girl, at least. She'll have to do." He dropped me back onto the ground, snatched up the sack, and strode out of the barn, slamming the door behind him.

The farmer left us there for several weeks, and my mother seemed grateful for the rest. I grew stronger each day as I nuzzled her, and she tried to feed me as best she could. Her own body was skin and bone, and she looked much older than her years. She had spent her whole life with a chain around her neck, tied to an old kennel outside.

Her only reprieve from the chain came when the farmer brought over one of the hunting dogs to mate with her. Once she got close to full term, he moved her inside the barn until the birth. He then inspected her offspring, selecting the strongest male. The others he carried off, and she never saw them again. This time, my mother knew she had failed him. A girl was no use to him. He wanted more male dogs to hunt with.

The morning arrived when he dragged my mother back outside and tied her up, dropping me on the ground beside her. Bruno, the farm dog, growled at us as the farmer untied him. He trotted away, glad to be relieved of his guard duties, I'm sure. My mother reached over and licked me as I curled up on the hard kennel floor and tried to sleep.

Several weeks passed, and I grew stronger and ventured out further into the yard each morning to sit and watch the chickens in their pen. My mother let me play in the spring sunshine, knowing what lay ahead. She was old and tired, and it took all her energy to stay awake at night to guard the livestock. Soon the farmer would come and carry her away and I would take her place.

But I knew none of that as I watched the chickens scurry around, flinging their feathers upwards as they scuffled with each other, fighting over the scraps of food that littered the floor.

The evening sun cast long ribbons of light across the concrete yard, and I sniffed the air. A mixture of peat and wood smoke filled my nose, together with something heavier and more sinister. Dark clouds loomed over the fields, hiding the moon from view. The branches of the trees whipped and bent as the wind whirled around, the timber creaking as I turned and huddled inside the kennel. I tucked myself in the far corner and tried to sleep. My mother spun round, trying to find a comfortable position on the cold concrete floor. There was barely room inside for both of us now. I had grown so much in a few short weeks.

The first drops of rain pounded onto the roof, and pellets of water bounced back up off the ground and skittered sideways. Soon the yard was soaking wet and still the pounding rain continued. Spring often heralded torrential downpours, the wind pushing the weather across the land in wave upon wave of stinging water, driving mercilessly over the fields. The rain drummed on, relentless, drowning out all sounds except the screaming wind.

My mother moved further into the kennel, away from the downpour, and fell into a deep and fitful sleep, her legs twitching as she dreamed. She did not hear the fox as he approached the farm, skirting the edge of the buildings, tucked into the shadows. He knew the weather would drown out any noise he made as he slunk across the yard, his nose quivering as he smelt the chickens huddled up in their makeshift wooden hut.

The metal fence gave way under his paws as he slithered underneath. The rain pounding onto his body didn't seem to bother him, as he shook his head and growled a low warning cry. I watched from inside the kennel. A gap between the wood panels offered me a perfect view out into the yard. I was too young to understand what was happening as I lay there in the darkness.

The chickens were flapping and scurrying inside the hut, trying to move away from the door as the fox stretched out a paw, extended his sharp claws and drew out his first victim. The chicken screeched out in pain, then fell silent, its neck snapped cleanly. Again and again, the fox slipped his paw inside and pulled out another victim.

Soon the floor was littered with bodies. Feathers stuck to the ground mingled with the blood spilling across the concrete. The rain continued to pound down as the wind picked up the scent of death and lifted it into the air. It reached my nose, and I twitched, the smell of hot raw blood and flesh pricking the back of my throat.

The fox picked up one bird and left the way he came, his paws padding over the courtyard as he slunk away into the field. My mother slept on, unaware of the carnage only a few feet away from her.

Early the next morning, the farmer walked outside. He sauntered over towards the barn, then uttered a loud cry as he saw the devastation in the chicken pen. Scrawny bodies with their heads severed lay in the mud, feathers whirled in the air, and the smell of blood hung heavy like a blanket.

The farmer turned and strode over to our kennel. My mother was still asleep, and I didn't even have time to warn her before he grabbed her collar and hauled her outside. He picked her up, twisting the collar until she yelped in pain. He untied her, throwing the chain to the ground, and marched over to the barn, dangling her by the scruff of her neck.

The farmer didn't see me crawl out from the back of the kennel. He carried my mother away around the corner, out of sight. I slunk back into the shadows, my body shaking.

The sound of gunfire echoed across the yard. In the field below, the crows perched in the oak trees pitched into the air, squawking and screeching their fury at being disturbed. They swooped right over my head, their cries filling the air, wings beating furiously. I squirmed backwards, desperate to escape the sinister birds, my heart pounding as they whirled and dipped in the sky overhead.

Suddenly, all was still and quiet. I shivered despite the morning sunshine as I waited. The farmer dragged a black bin bag over to the coop; the contents bumping along the ground as he walked. He picked up the dead chickens and tossed them into the bag, hosed down the pen, threw the bag into the back of his pickup truck and drove away.

CHAPTER TWO

"Luna," boomed the farmer as he marched over to the kennel. "I'll call you Luna." I winced as he picked me up and looped something over my head. *What's that? And where's my mother?* I had sat all morning in the same spot, waiting for her to return.

I squirmed, trying to shake my head out of the band secured around my neck. It pinched into my skin, and I did not like it.

The farmer dropped me to the ground, and I ran, struggling to get away from him. He frightened me with his loud voice and rough hands. My legs cycled forward, and I sped away, until, unexpectedly, my body jerked backwards. *Ouch! I must be caught on something.* I twisted round. The ring fastened to my neck was now attached to the metal chain tied to the wall. *I'm trapped.* The chain rattled and held fast. I writhed and wriggled to free myself, but it was no use.

I tried to work out how far I could walk. *I can make it into the kennel and over to the chicken pen. That's all.* My claws scrabbled on the hard ground as I twisted my neck from side to side. I lay down, dropping my head in defeat between my paws. *So I am to be called Luna.* I let the name sink in slowly.

"You'll guard the chickens now," said the farmer, as he left a bowl of water for me and walked away.

I never saw my mother again. The days got longer, and summer came. It was stifling hot and the only shade I could find was inside the kennel. The farmer had fashioned the sides out of an old wooden crate with a sheet of plastic for a roof. When it rained, water pooled on one side, and in the summer, the cover made it almost as hot inside as out in the yard.

I quickly realised what my job was. Every time someone or something approached my kennel, I had to bark. At night, I was there to protect the chickens from intruders. Each tiny noise, the rustle of the grass, the distant creak of the trees in the field, set me on edge. Sometimes the snickering call of the foxes reached me as they roamed the surrounding land. I would lie quietly, listening, waiting to leap up and bark a warning cry if they came too close. I remembered what had happened to my mother and tried to stay alert.

At least at night, the farmer never bothered me. One morning, I was dozing in the sunshine and didn't hear him until he was almost beside me. I leapt up and barked, but it was too late. He grabbed my collar and dragged me to my feet, then picked up a broom lying on the ground nearby.

As the first strike hit my back, I yelped as a sharp sting of pain shot through my legs. I bowed my head and curled up, trying to avoid the blows, as he sliced the wooden stick down again and again.

"That will remind you to bark when someone comes near." He threw down the broom and strode away.

I crawled into the kennel and tried to lick my wounds, shivering and whimpering with pain. My back throbbed and burned for days afterwards. I never missed his approach again, leaping up into the air and barking wildly as soon as I saw him. He was erratic, though, and I never knew when he was going to hit me. I grew to hate that broom and often walked with a limp for weeks after his beatings.

The chickens were my only companions. I watched them for hours each day as they preened themselves in their pen, which was now bordered by a new wire mesh fence. They pecked the ground, looking for the tiniest grain of food, squabbling and squawking over the meagre supply of corn and leafy stalks the farmer threw over the fence for them. The cockerel strutted around, batting the younger chickens out of his path, and crowing loudly. The first time I heard his screeching cry, I nearly jumped out of my skin. After a while, I got used to him firing his morning wake-up call as soon as the first rays of sunlight peeped over the distant hills.

The farm was a tired-looking collection of ruined and crumbling buildings, set amidst a concrete courtyard. The farmer had stacked old pallets of wood against the barn wall and a rusting tractor lay collapsed in a heap beside the farmhouse. Weeds had grown through the wheels, weaving their way upwards, spiralling into the sunshine undisturbed. An old rope strung between two trees served as a washing line, and an assortment of discarded oil drums were balanced beside the rickety gate that led to the field beyond the farm.

Some nights, I hid in the shadows as the farmer came outside, greeting the world with a loud belch as he threw another empty beer bottle into the bushes. He would stagger round, kicking plant pots aside and tossing bags of rubbish across the yard. I buried myself away inside my kennel when he was in that kind of mood.

One morning, Bruno, the farm dog, appeared, circling around the side of the shed. I shrank back, hoping he would ignore me as he usually did. But this time he marched straight up to me, and I lowered my head, unsure of what he wanted. He pushed me against the wall and mounted me, then scampered off, leaving me dazed and sore. A few weeks later, a slight flutter stirred inside me, like a butterfly caught in a net, and then I knew what had happened.

The farmer didn't seem to notice anything different until one day he spotted my swollen belly.

"How on earth did that happen?" he roared, as he untied me and threw me into the toolshed, locking the door.

I lay in the darkness, whimpering until it was time. Soon I had four pups surrounding me, all clambering to be fed, sucking noisily on my teats. I sunk back against the wall exhausted, as an overwhelming feeling of love and pride filled my heart. Deep inside, an instant bond formed, a thread of pure tenderness that reached out and wrapped itself around each pup. The same thread that had woven back through my own mother and her mother before her. It was primeval and wonderful, an attraction that drew me to my babies as surely as I lifted my head to face the sun each morning.

I licked each one, marvelling at how quickly they had been born, and how keen they were to feed. I curled up, tucking them into my belly, and fell asleep.

The sound of the shed door crashing open woke me. The farmer loomed over me, his face scrunched up, eyes glaring. He had left me alone with my pups for almost four weeks, bringing in food and water each day. His gaze hardened as he snatched up one of the wriggling pups. He dismissed her, tossing her to the floor. She mewed like a cat, and I instinctively moved to protect her, releasing the others from my grasp.

The farmer picked up each pup, spinning them in the air, then dropping them with a thud until he came to the last one, a healthy boy. He seemed satisfied with this one, placing him gently on the ground. Before I could do anything, he grabbed the other three, holding them dangling by their necks, and marched out of the shed, slamming the door shut.

The remaining pup cried out, opening his mouth wide in hunger. I let him nuzzle me as I stared at the door, torn between wanting to go after my other pups, and knowing I had to feed and protect the one left beside me. The whole incident was over so fast I didn't even have time to react. I refused to admit that deep inside, I knew something was wrong.

The hours passed, and still the farmer didn't return with my other pups. A dark and heavy weight descended into my heart as I realised what had happened. I dragged myself into a corner and collapsed, my whole body shaking as I curled up into a ball.

A few days later, the farmer turfed me out of the shed. He tied me up beside my kennel, tossing the remaining pup on the ground alongside me. I tried to make him comfortable and licked him all over, trying to reassure him everything was alright. He grew strong as the days passed. He was beautiful, with caramel eyes that were bright and alert, and a long swishy tail.

When he was only seven weeks old, the farmer picked him up one morning, his puppy legs dangling as he gave a pitiful, mewling cry. The farmer walked away, carrying my boy under his arm. I tried to follow, but the chain caught me as I pulled and pulled, the collar tightening around my neck until I could hardly breathe. My boy's whimpering cries haunted me as they faded into the distance.

I never saw him again, but I heard him bark sometimes. The hunting dogs were in their own kennels on the far side of the farm. Their yelps and cries filled the air as the farmer fed them each morning. Once a week, he released them, herding them into small pens on the back of his pickup truck. Their howls of excitement reached a fever pitch as the farmer drove past me. I knew my pup was in there somewhere, and I hoped they had accepted him as part of the pack.

But I never forgot the other pups from that litter. Sometimes on a clear moonlit night, I would look up and imagine that each one was a star twinkling in the sky.

CHAPTER THREE

The next time Bruno came skulking past my kennel, I tried hard to avoid him, but it was in vain. He was bigger than me and much more powerful. He left me lying shattered, my breath coming out in ragged gasps as I curled up and attempted to block out the memory of him attacking me.

Once again, a few weeks later, the same fluttering stirred inside me and I hung my head in shame. This time I knew what was coming and being led into the shed was a relief. I was free of the chain around my neck, and I settled down in the straw, my belly bursting. After the pups were born, I hatched a plan. I had three beautiful strong girls, and when I heard the farmer's footsteps approaching, I hid them in the corner of the shed. But my poor babies hated being away from the warmth of my body and whimpered as he entered the shed and searched for them. They were all dragged out, picked up, and thrown into a sack on the ground. He hefted a kick in my direction, grunting as he hoisted up the sack. He marched out, slamming the door behind him.

Alone in the shed, a darkness descended inside me. *I'm so sorry I couldn't protect you. Please forgive me,* I whispered to myself as I wrapped my paws under my body, shivering despite the warm evening air.

The farmer placed me back in my kennel on the chain, and I huddled into a ball. My body was heavy as lead, and my teats dried up like concrete. It was almost too much effort to move, even to eat or drink, as I lay there wishing he had thrown me into the sack with my babies. That night, I dreamt my mother was with me. She lay in the kennel beside me and nuzzled me, licking away my tears, then wrapped herself around me, murmuring words of love. In the morning I woke, hoping to find her still there, but she had gone.

I stirred and rose slowly. Stretching my legs out, I glanced up at the sky. The sun was just rising over the hills, painting brushstrokes of deep pink through the clouds, and the air was still. *I'm alive. If this is to be my life, so be it.*

But something changed in me after that day. I plodded up and down, barking when I had to, and eating my food. But there was no joy in my heart. Just a heaviness, a solid weight that draped across me, constantly dragging me down. I used to view the world through the eyes of a pup, full of wonder and delight at each new day. Now I felt old and defeated, resigned to the fact I would spend my days and nights tied to a wall.

The only bright moments occurred when the farmer's family came to visit. Sometimes a young girl was with them, and she would come outside and play with me. The farmer let her unhook me and she walked me round the farm, holding onto an old lead she found in the shed. I enjoyed the freedom of being released from the chain, and the girl let me stop and sniff the ground. So many tantalising smells filled my nose as I took in deep breaths of air, lifting my head high to catch the breeze as it swept past me.

We walked to the edge of the farm, and I stared through the fence at the field below, wondering what it would be like to run through the grass. But we didn't leave the yard, and all too soon she returned me to the kennel and tied me up again.

I had two more litters over the years that followed, and I lost track of time. My only way of knowing another year had passed was each spring the farmer dragged me into the cowshed and trimmed off all my fur. Black curls tumbled to the floor as I stood there on a low table, the silver machine humming as he passed it over my body.

I shook all over the first time it happened, not knowing what to expect, as the farmer grabbed me by the scruff of my neck and dragged me across to the shed. His hands gripped my legs as he sheared me like a sheep, but the relief afterwards, once all my thick fur had gone, was astonishing. I could move freely, my legs fluttering with each step, no longer burdened by a thick winter coat.

One afternoon, the young girl skipped towards me, twirling the lead in her hands.

"Come on Luna, let's go for a walk."

We wandered around the farm and even went behind the cowshed, where I had never been before. I slowed down as we strolled past the kennels with the hunting dogs. They barked and howled at us, lunging at the fence in a frenzy of paws and snarls. I peered at each face, trying to see if my boy was amongst them, but I couldn't spot him.

We ambled back to my kennel, as the farmer shouted, "Hurry Amy, we're going to be late." She unhooked the lead from my collar, her fingers stumbling to reattach the chain before she ran over to her family. I lay down. It had been so nice to go for a walk. I moved position to settle in a patch of sunshine. It was spring, and the sun was warm enough to ease my aching body.

I rolled over, then looked behind me in surprise. Something was missing. I had grown so used to hearing a clank and rattle each time I moved that the silence was eerie. The chain lay coiled up beside my kennel; the metal glinting in the sunshine. In her haste to leave, with fumbling fingers, the girl had not clipped it to my collar.

Now what do I do? The farmer's family piled into their car and drove away, horns blaring, hands waving from the open windows. A few minutes later, the farmer picked up his gun, released one of the hunting dogs who jumped in the rear of the pickup, and they left in a squeal of tyres and dust. He had gone in search of rabbits and I knew he wouldn't be back for hours.

I stared at the chain furled up on the ground. Now was my chance. *But how can I leave? Isn't it my job to stay here and protect the chickens? Where will I go?* My mind raced as I struggled to decide what to do. A shadow cast over me as Bruno appeared round the corner, blocking the sun. He was surefooted as he ambled over towards me, and my heart sank. Suddenly, a crashing noise came from the cowshed and Bruno turned and went to investigate, his tail high in the air.

I decided there and then he would never attack me again. I waited until he had gone round the corner, then I darted away, not daring to look back. I picked up speed and raced to the fence, squeezing through a gap in the panels. My breath came in rasping gasps as I slowed down and glanced behind me. All was quiet. *I've done it. I've escaped.*

The sunlight cast patterns on the land as I pattered across the field, the ground springy beneath my paws. It was the first time I had ever walked on grass. The silky green feathers tickled my back as I stopped to roll over, lifting my legs in the air, the sun warm on my belly. I was free. The weight I had been carrying each day disappeared as I jiggled from side to side, wriggling in delight. I ate a few blades of grass, and it was the sweetest thing I had ever tasted.

I scampered over to the far side of the field, the farm receding into the distance. A small river trickled and gurgled in front of me. I scrambled down the bank and bent my head to drink the cold, fresh water. It splashed up my nose as I gulped mouthfuls of the icy liquid.

I followed a path that meandered beside the river, padding through the soft soil. The smells were different here, earthy and fresh, and enticing. The trees lining the river were so tall their trunks almost touched the sky, their leaves whirling and whispering in the breeze. I sat below a tree in blossom and listened to a blackbird perched on a branch as he sang, chirruping and whistling to his mate. I closed my eyes and drifted to sleep, a sense of peace I had never experienced before filling my soul.

The sound of scuffling nearby startled me out of my slumber. A hedgehog was rustling through the roots of the trees, busily snuffling for food. He shuffled through the undergrowth, making plenty of noise, as he flicked the grass and leaves aside. He was oblivious to me as he scurried along. A twig cracked, and he halted, his nose twitching. His head shot back into his body and he was still. I sniffed him tentatively, a voice in my head warning me not to get too close to the spines quivering in front of me.

My belly growled. *Where am I going to find some food?*

The path wound its way upward until it opened out into a wide concrete space with cars parked on either side. I hid in the shadows behind a low wall and waited. There was no one around. I edged out slowly, eventually coming to a set of bins tucked in the corner. I found an open packet with a half-eaten sandwich and gulped it down. It tasted salty, and I licked the container. I hadn't eaten for hours. I searched around, but there was no more food to be found.

I needed to make a decision. I certainly couldn't return to the farm, and I wanted to get as far away from there as possible. A paved road led off from the car park, and twinkling lights lit up the sky in the distance. I circled back to the river and waited. As dusk approached, I picked up the path again and set off towards the lights.

CHAPTER FOUR

It was dark by the time I reached the village and the source of the lights. I shuffled around for a while, trying to understand the layout and not wanting anyone to see me. I wandered down an alleyway, keeping close to the wall. Ahead of me was a set of bins, the same colour as the ones I had found earlier. *Maybe there will be food there?*

I was so hungry my stomach was churning and contracting. The farmer had never given me much to eat, but each evening he had put out a bowl of scraps, which I devoured. *Have I made a mistake leaving the farm? At least I had food and shelter there.*

I stepped forward, my ears alert to the slightest sound. I sniffed the air. Old rotting meat. I found a plastic container lying beside the bins. Just as I nudged my nose inside it, a door opened into the lane. Light spilled out and a young man appeared outside, carrying a large bin bag. I jumped and tried to hide, sliding backwards into the shadows.

"Hello, little one. It's okay, I won't hurt you." He held out his hand.

"You look hungry," he said, opening the bag. "Let's see what we're throwing away that you can eat."

He pulled out some scraps of meat and placed them on the ground. He backed away and stood with his arms folded. It smelt so good I risked it and edged out, walking towards the food. I scoffed the lot, checking around me several times as I gulped it down.

"Hang on there. I'll bring out some more." As he opened the door and went inside, I glimpsed a kitchen and smelt food frying. He returned a few minutes later with a metal bowl, which he put down for me. Chicken scraps and bones. I crept over and ate everything as fast as I could.

A few minutes later, an older man came out carrying a wooden box.

"What's that doing here?" he said and aimed a kick at me. I shot backwards, as the edge of his foot skimmed across my rear. I whimpered and tried to tuck myself in behind the bins.

"Oh, don't hurt her. She's just hungry. See how skinny she is?" the young man replied.

"Well, she can't hang around here. If the boss catches her, he'll go mad." He stooped down and snatched up a rock, then sent it spinning towards me. It bounced off the bin beside me.

"Go on, shoo! Get away from here."

I slid out, keeping my back to the wall, then ran off, the man's words ringing in my ears.

🐾 🐾 🐾 🐾 🐾

I headed towards a deserted patch of land beside the road. The grass was damp, and I licked it, longing for a bowl of fresh water to drink. I found a corner and fell into an uneasy sleep. A dog barked in the distance and cars drove past, their engines whirring. It was so different from the farm, and each time I heard a strange noise, I awoke with a start.

Morning arrived early as I stretched and yawned. People were moving around and there were more cars whizzing along the road. I needed to find somewhere quieter. I walked to the edge of the village and found a house tucked away at the end of a lane. A family came outside into the garden, two children playing together, as a lady hung out their washing. I edged closer.

"Look Mom, a little dog!"

The young girl ran over to me, and I lingered in front of the gate. I liked her. She was smiling, and I sensed she wouldn't hurt me.

"Can we play with her?" She patted me on the head, her chubby hands reaching through the gate and softly cupping my ears. "She looks hungry. Can we feed her?"

Her mother walked over and looked at me. I lowered my head and waited, expecting her to shout at me.

"She is a skinny thing. I'll see what scraps we have left over, but we're going home tomorrow. And no, before you ask, we can't take her with us."

"Oh, Mom."

"No, 'Oh Mom'. And that's final. But we can feed her today. She might just be lost. I'm sure she has a home somewhere." She walked off towards the house as the older girl opened the gate.

I tiptoed into the garden, still wary of them, and checked she hadn't locked the gate behind me. I wanted to make sure my escape route was intact.

The lady came out carrying a plate of food. It smelt wonderful as I sidled up to it and sniffed. Ham and cheese. I swallowed it all in three giant gulps, then licked the plate.

"Well, you were hungry," the mother said and laughed. "I'll see if I can find some more for you."

She returned with another plate of meat and a bowl of water. I ate it all and slurped up the water, my tongue snaking over my lips to catch the last slivers of food. The little girl was watching me. I walked over to her and sat at her feet.

"Can she stay here today? Please, Mom? She looks tired. She needs to sleep."

"Yes, I'll put an old blanket down for her. But we're off tomorrow, so she'll have to leave then. We won't be here until next spring. And no, she can't come with us. So don't ask me again."

The mother walked over to a wooden shed and laid a rug on the floor. She called me over and left the door ajar. I lay on the rug and fell asleep, my stomach bloated.

It was hours later before I woke up, unsure of where I was for a moment. Someone had placed another bowl of water for me beside the door and I drank thirstily. Venturing outside, I peered my head around the wall, but there was no-one there.

I lay in the sunshine for a while until a car approached the house. I dashed behind a hedge, carefully hiding myself away, and held my breath. The family climbed out of the car and the little girl ran to the shed, then cried out, "She's not here."

I stepped forward a pace, wary of the tall man stood with them.

"There she is, over there," he said, pointing at me. His voice was reassuring, as he stretched out his fingers, gesturing for me to come towards him.

The girl bounded over and stroked my head. I had never been touched so gently before and I rolled over and showed her my tummy. She giggled and rubbed me with long, soothing strokes as I reclined and enjoyed the sensation of her hand caressing me.

They fed me again, then left me in the shed as night fell. I curled up into a ball and slept soundly. The next morning, the parents were bustling in and out of the house carrying bags and boxes that they put in the boot of their car. The girls were told off several times for getting in the way.

"Sorry old girl," the man said, as he saw me watching him. "We're off home today, and you can't come with us. You'll have to find somewhere else to live. Or go back to where you came from." He folded up the blanket, placed it on a shelf, and locked up the shed.

I didn't really understand what was happening as they climbed into the car and drove off. The little girl waved to me as they turned the corner and sped away. I sat in the garden for ages, hoping they would come back.

It was dark before I realised they were not going to return. I trudged back to the alleyway, but when I got there, it was in darkness, and no-one came out of the doors that night. I found an old bin bag and snuffled inside, finding a few mouldy scraps of bread to eat. I hunched up in the corner and eventually drifted off to sleep.

CHAPTER FIVE

I wandered around the village for months, hiding in the shadows and only venturing out when I needed to eat. I was constantly hungry and had lost weight. Every day, I tried to find food, but it wasn't always easy. The pads on my paws became cracked and split. Walking on the hot pavements and concrete made them so sore. My legs ached, and I spent hours licking them each night, trying to ease the pain.

I learnt to keep away from the park in the afternoon. Once the local school finished for the day, children would stream through the gates, bags tumbling to the ground, screams and shouts breaking the silence. Some of them would kick a football around and I wandered over to watch one day, drawn by their joyful cries and laughter. One boy gestured to me, and I padded over towards him and his outstretched hand, sniffing the air. The sickly sweet aroma of candy bars and sweat mingled together, making me shudder.

As I got closer, his voice dropped to a menacing grunt, and I stepped back. His hand shot in the air as he tried to grab my collar. I growled, baring my teeth, suddenly afraid. He lunged for me and missed, toppling over. He righted himself and cursed, reaching for a stick lying nearby. The other boys came over and joined in, picking up rocks and stones as I raced off, my heart pounding.

One afternoon, an old lady spoke to me. Her voice sounded soft, and I was desperate for food, so I followed her home. She opened the gate to a cottage and beckoned me inside. There was a wooden porch, and I perched on the step, keeping an eye on the gate.

The lady came outside carrying a bowl of water and a handful of meat, and I sat still as she fed me. She placed a rug onto an old wicker chair in the corner and said to me, "There you are. You can sleep here if you want to."

I hopped onto the chair. My eyes fluttered, then closed. She touched my back, and I shot to my feet, startled, but her voice was soothing as she stroked me.

"Oh, don't jump, little one. I won't hurt you. You are a scared skinny thing, aren't you? Go to sleep now; you're safe here."

I must have fallen asleep, as I awoke hours later, just as the sun was setting over the hills in the distance. The cottage was at the far end of the village, set on the top of the hill above the roofs of the other houses. The main road stretched below us in the shape of a lizard, snaking its way down to the valley, where a low mist was settling like a thin sheet of gauze on the horizon. Distant church bells chimed. Pots planted with lavender were scattered around the porch, the heady perfume hanging in the air, and all was peaceful.

The old lady settled herself in a recliner opposite me, rocking gently. Her chair squeaked slightly as it moved, making me jump the first time I heard it. I licked my paws, trying to clean myself up a little, as the lady sat reading quietly. The rhythmic squeak of the chair stopped as she fell asleep, her book slipping down to her side as her hands fluttered. I wondered what she was dreaming about.

She wore an apron stretched over her skirt, her thick stockings were bunched at the ankles, feet stuffed into a fluffy pair of slippers. Her faded blue blouse was old and well-worn, and her face was open and friendly. A wool cardigan slipped off her shoulders as her soft snores broke the silence.

Dinner time came, and she woke up, stretching and yawning. I went out into the lane, not wishing to do my business in her garden. She called me and I returned to the porch, just as she set down another plate of food and a bowl of fresh water. I ate it all, then curled up on the chair and fell asleep listening to the sound of an owl hooting in a nearby tree.

I spent several days with her. The lady seemed to enjoy my company as we slipped into an easy routine. I wandered along the lanes near the cottage during the day, returning each afternoon to sit beside her on the porch. She fed me every morning and evening, and I slept on the chair each night.

Then one day, everything changed. A man pulled up in a car outside. The old lady tugged her cardigan tighter around her shoulders, her hands shaking. She peeked over at me, but before she could say anything, the man strode over towards us.

"Good morning, Mother." He kissed her cheek, then glanced over and saw me. I felt the hairs on my back prickle as his voice dropped menacingly low. "What's that doing there?"

"Oh, she's alright. Don't worry." The old lady's voice wavered as she moved to stand in front of me. I sat up in the chair behind her, ready to move in an instant.

The man pushed past her, and I leapt off the chair, but he was too quick for me, and his boot grazed my back leg as I squirmed past him. I yelped as he yelled, "Go on, get out of here!"

I ran to the gate, then turned back. The lady sank down into her armchair, shoulders slumped forwards. I had never seen her looking so frail and helpless.

"The little dog wasn't doing any harm. She was keeping me company," she murmured, clenching a handkerchief in her hands.

"Well, you can't keep her. You can barely look after yourself anymore. It's time you agreed to go into that nice home I found for you, instead of living here on your own."

She made a small gasping noise as I limped away. I never saw her again. I walked past the cottage a few days later, but everything was quiet. The window shutters were all closed, and the chairs were no longer on the porch.

I was still wearing the collar the farmer had placed around my neck, and it was to be my undoing. The village had a series of cafés and shops all set around a main square and as time passed and winter approached, I grew more desperate for food and company. I discovered that later in the afternoon, once the lunchtime rush was over, the tables in front of the cafés usually had remnants of food scattered underneath them. Often the waiting staff stayed inside unless a customer appeared, and if I was quick enough, I could whisk around the tables and snatch up the scraps of food.

A man appeared in the village every day, shuffling along carrying a bucket. He looped his arm through the handle, and the bucket bumped against his side with every step he took. I peered inside it one day when he wasn't looking, but it was empty. It was most strange.

The man was obviously hungry as he sat each day on a bench in the square begging for money. I sat and watched from a distance as he settled himself down, placing an old battered flat cap upside down on the pavement. People left the cafés after lunch, their stomachs full of food, laughing and chatting, and walked past the man. He held out his hand and stared out into the distance, as if he was blind. I guess the people felt sorry for him, or perhaps they felt guilty after their big lunches, but either way, they often dropped a few coins or a note into his hat. He would touch his forehead with his finger, then reach down and grab the money, stuffing it into his pocket.

I wish I had a hat I could put on the ground. Maybe if I sit next to him, someone might take pity on me too and give me some food. I thought about my plan for a few days, not wanting to risk getting too close to him, but eventually my stomach growled so loudly that I ventured out and wandered over towards him.

He didn't see me at first as I dived under the tables of one of the cafés and wolfed down a stray piece of pastry. It was sweet and buttery, and I licked my lips, scouting around to see if there was any more. I edged up to him, my nose curling as the smell of urine and musty papers reached me.

He was wearing an old pair of trousers that were too short for his legs, the waist wrapped around with a piece of thin rope. His shoes were scuffed and covered in dried earth, the laces tatty and knotted. A faded, patched jacket covered several layers of shirts and jumpers, all with holes in different places, and a bundle of string tumbled out of one of his pockets. He smelt as if he hadn't washed in a very long time, and the stink of tobacco smoke had settled on his clothes like a stale mist swirling around him. I almost ran away at that moment as the smell transported me instantly back to the farm in my mind. The farmer always had that same sickly stench of old smoke seeping through his clothes, cloying and acrid.

I shook my head from side to side as fusty mould and stale body odour, mixed with something sour, reached my nose. No wonder no-one got too close to the man. He smelt awful. But hunger won, and I crept nearer. The man stared at me as I sat down a few paces away from him and waited.

A young woman crossed the square and came towards us. I shrank back, but she marched over and stopped in front of me.

"Ahh, what a sweet little dog. She looks hungry. Here, have some money to buy her some food." The woman dropped a note into the man's hat, then walked away, her shoes clacking on the pavement as she left.

The man seized the note before the wind could whirl it away. His hands were gnarled and dirty, caked with grime and grease, as he held the note up to his face and smiled. I noticed he was missing several teeth. His grin was lopsided, almost a snarl.

"Ten euros. Good dog. You might come in handy. Get over here and let me have a look at you."

I tried to shrink away, but he reached over and grabbed me by the collar, twisting my head as he pulled me towards him. Before I knew it, he had pulled the rope from his pocket and looped it under my collar, tying it in a knot.

"You sit down here beside me and look cute. You can earn your keep and I'll feed you later."

I had no choice. I collapsed to the ground, resting my head on my paws, and tried not to panic. *Maybe it will be alright. He said he would feed me.* I tried to sleep, but every time I closed my eyes, he yanked hard on the rope, hoisting me back up to my feet.

"Sit up. Look hungry. The punters are going to love you."

What have I done?

CHAPTER SIX

The light was fading as the man finally lurched to his feet, grasped his bucket and yanked me up, tugging on the rope to test the knot he had made. It held firm, and I had no alternative but to walk off beside him. He stopped in front of a grocery shop, tying the rope up to a metal ring on the wall and wove his way inside.

The lady at the till seemed to know him as she reached down under the counter and pulled out two shiny metal cans and a packet of cigarettes, placing them in the bucket. She added a packet of sandwiches and the man paid and came back outside and untied me.

He staggered off down the road, clutching the rope, as I dragged my paws along, trying to loosen the knot around my collar. It was impossible. The man had a limp, and the bucket clanked as he walked, the cans inside clattering together with each jolting step he took. We turned down a side lane, and the pavement turned to mud as we squeezed through a gap in a fence. Ahead was an old tumbledown abandoned house, with half its roof missing. Beside it was a shed, with a corrugated metal roof, the battered wooden door hanging grimly by a rusting metal hinge.

The man kicked an old paint tin aside as he lurched through the door, pulling me inside the shed behind him. A faint line of light from a hole in the roof snaked across the concrete floor, which was strewn with old newspapers and empty cloth sacks. Garden tools hung from the walls, ominous sharp metal spikes and shovels that made me shudder. *I don't like this place.*

The man yanked me forward and tied the end of the rope to a metal handle jutting out from the wall. I sank to the floor, my legs aching and my stomach twisting with hunger. He reached into the bucket and grabbed a can, pulling the ring on the top. The man gasped as he drank deeply from the can, wiping his mouth with his hand as he finished. A sweet, sickly smell wafted over to me. *I hope he doesn't get angry the same as the farmer used to after drinking that stuff.*

He pulled out the packet of sandwiches. I sat up, licking my lips, the aroma of ham making me shiver as he pulled open the wrapper. He shovelled the food into his mouth, spitting out crumbs of bread as he chewed loudly. He ate the lot. I blinked. *Surely, he's left some for me?* There was nothing. He slurped up the rest of the can of drink, rolled over, and fell asleep. Soon, his snores filled the shed, rattling off the walls as I sat there in dismay. *I need to get away from here.*

Morning finally came as the man grunted and rolled over. He sat up, scratching his side, and picked at his teeth with a long dirty fingernail. The sour odour that surrounded him was even stronger this morning as he lunged to his feet and gripped my collar, untying the rope from the wall.

"Time to go. Let's find some breakfast and see how many people fall for your charms today."

I found a puddle and licked up the drops of water as we walked to the square, then huddled down under the bench as the man arranged his hat on the ground. A family walked by and stopped to give him some money. The young boy with them gave me a chunk of pastry, dropping it at my feet and patted my head. I snatched it up and scoffed it quickly, feeling my stomach contract as the food slipped down my throat.

A waiter appeared from a café and waved his tea towel at us, shouting at the man to go away. Another man came outside and joined in.

"Go sit somewhere else. We don't want you begging outside here all day. Go and get a job. And take your scruffy dog with you."

They went back inside, and the man muttered to himself, clutched his bucket and pulled me away. We walked over to the other side of the square and he perched on the wall of a flowerbed, bending over to rifle through the plants. He picked up the nub end of a cigarette and lit it, drawing deeply for one puff before the end died, then threw it to the ground.

We spent all day moving around the square and into the park, being shooed away and settling somewhere else, the man always pleading for money. Enough people walked by dropping scraps of food for me, so I didn't starve. A shop even had a bowl of water outside and I drank deeply. The cool, fresh liquid was like velvet as I licked up every drop.

The days and weeks blurred into an endless nightmare. Each day, the same round of begging, walking, and scrounging food. I spent my nights huddled up in the shed, listening to the man snoring and groaning in his sleep. Winter came and the money in the hat dried up as the man took to grovelling at the back doors of the restaurants at the end of the night. Sometimes the staff threw out leftover food, and I would devour everything as quickly as I could before the man could stop me. He spent all his money on beer, often sitting in the park with another man, drinking until he could hardly walk back to the shed.

One evening, as we sat in the park, a man lurched over towards us.

"Carlos, old man. How are you? And what's that you've got there? I didn't know you had a dog."

"Evening, Miguel. Long time no see. Yes, I've got a dog now. She adopted me."

I watched with interest. My homeless man didn't exactly seem pleased to see the other man as he crashed down on the bench beside him.

"Got any beers?"

They sat drinking until it was dark, then staggered to their feet, swaying and singing.

"I think I'll come back with you tonight. Stay in your shed. And drink more beer."

I trudged back with them. It didn't seem to matter how drunk the man was; he never loosened his grip on the rope tied around my neck. I hung my head low. I wouldn't be eating anything tonight if they were busy drinking.

They crashed into the shed door, almost knocking it off its remaining hinge, leaving it hanging lopsided. It looked as drunk as the two men as it dangled there, swaying and creaking. The man dropped his bucket to the ground and tied me to the wall, muttering to himself.

"I must find a new rope tomorrow. This one is frayed."

My ears pricked up. *That sounds promising. I wonder if I can finally break free and escape this madness?*

They carried on drinking and smoking as I lay down and tried to sleep. It was impossible.

"Here, why does your dog have such a stubby tail? What happened to it?"

"No idea. She just turned up one day looking like that. She's great with the punters though, they take pity on her and give me more money. I'm supposed to buy food for her." A bitter laugh followed by a fit of coughing and wheezing stopped him talking for a minute.

"But I like to keep her looking skinny and hungry. It's better for me."

"D'you think someone cut off her tail, then?" The other man reached over and tried to grab me as I pulled away from him. "I know. Let's set fire to what's left of her tail and watch it burn." He grinned and reached for his lighter.

I shrank back in horror. The man lunged for me but fell over, rolling around laughing. Bile rose in my throat.

"Nah, leave her be. Come on, last tinny each."

They grabbed their drinks, and I slunk down into the shadows. Eventually, they fell asleep, slumped on the floor, snoring like wild animals. I waited for a while, until I was sure they were both unconscious, then stood and strained forward. The collar round my neck cut into my skin as I stretched and pulled at the rope tied to the wall.

The nylon cord squeaked as it tore, piece by piece, slowly giving way as I twisted and turned. I bent my head in one last desperate attempt. White spots danced across my eyes as I lurched forward, almost choking. I crashed to the ground, panting. I was free.

I shook myself and checked around. They were both still fast asleep. I sneaked out of the barn, sliding through the gate dangling on its hinge, and raced off into the darkness.

CHAPTER SEVEN

After that, I kept to the fields surrounding the village, not wanting to encounter anyone else that might hurt me. I knew the drunk man's routine and kept well away from his haunts. There was a small car park at the entrance to some woods with two metal bins and picnic tables set on the grass. It was now spring and most days there was some food scattered on the floor, and the river was nearby for water. I passed the time quietly, watching the people come and go, tucking myself into the shadows. I had fashioned a den near the trees, digging out the soil in a shaded corner.

Families sometimes came and set up a picnic at the site, children squealing and dancing around. They would cover the table with food and drinks, their laughter and chatter filling the air, and I would creep up to the edge of the car park and watch them. I knew I would eat well after they had gone. Children always dropped food under the table. I wondered if they even knew I was there or realised how grateful I was.

One afternoon, a lady arrived and parked up. Three dogs bolted out of her car and raced around before all setting off for a walk through the woods with her. I watched, longing to join the dogs as they bounded off, barking in delight. They returned much later, panting and scuffling each other as they bent their heads to drink water from a bowl the lady had placed on the ground. I could smell the meaty biscuits she fed them from my hiding place, and I stepped forward out of the shadows, drawn by the enticing aroma of the food.

The dogs jumped up into the boot. The lady picked up the water bowl, then saw me standing nearby. I hesitated, wondering what she would do.

"Hello, you do look a sight. I bet you're hungry. D'you want a biscuit?"

My mouth dribbled as I thought about how tasty it would be, but I held back, uncertain.

She threw a biscuit onto the ground and I slunk forward, keeping my eyes on her as I snatched it up. Another biscuit followed, but then she took a step towards me, and I turned and ran back to the safety of the trees.

"Poor thing. I'll come back later and see if I can find you again."

The car engine roared into life as she drove off. I stayed hidden for hours, not venturing out. As darkness snuffed out the last of the daylight, a vehicle drove into the car park and doors slammed shut. I huddled further down inside my den.

I heard distant voices, two people, both walking around.

"He was around here. He raced off and I couldn't stop him."

"Maybe he's gone home. He was probably just hungry. Come on, we can't do anything else if we can't find him."

They got back in their car and drove away. I sat pondering over their words. *They must have been talking about me. They thought I was a boy. I guess my long fur made it difficult for them to see I'm a girl.*

I looked at my coat, my curls now tangled and matted. The hair round my eyes had grown so long it was difficult for me to see where I was going, and the fur under my belly was full of burrs. I tried to pull them out with my teeth, but they were woven in tightly, fastened around my curls like tiny hedgehogs hooked into my fleece. My skin itched too. I knew I must have a collection of fleas and other crawling creatures nested in my fur, but there was nothing I could do about them. No wonder that lady had driven away.

Summer came, and the days were long as butterflies danced across the grass and the birds twittered in the trees. They all seemed to have something to do, and I was all alone and bored.

One morning I woke and stretched out my legs, the sunshine already warm on my back. My body felt peculiar, heavier, sluggish. I was in season. I licked myself clean, knowing I smelt different, pungent, and dangerous. There were other stray dogs in the village, but they rarely bothered me. I burrowed into a hole behind a tree and tried to conceal myself. But it was to no avail. Within a few hours, a couple of male dogs started circling round the edge of the car park. They went away as I hid further into the woods. I stayed still for as long as I could, until hunger got the better of me and I crept out, skirting the boundary of the field until I reached the bins.

I snuffled my nose into a discarded plastic bag and then heard a twig crack behind me. My body stiffened, and I twisted round, coming face to face with another black dog that looked just like me. He had soft curly fur, hazel brown eyes and a short stubby tail that wagged lazily. He greeted me, sniffing my nose, and I turned my back to greet him. We circled each other, and he nuzzled me. It was the first time I had ever encountered another dog that was nice to me, and I dropped my head, allowing him to sniff me.

After that, it was inevitable he would follow me to my den, and he settled down on the floor. He didn't seem to be in a hurry as he licked his paws, and I wriggled in beside him, happy for the company. Later that evening he climbed onto me, and I let him, enjoying the warm closeness of his body. It was so different from Bruno, the farm dog, and I fell asleep afterwards, snuggling into my new friend.

In the morning he had gone, and I busied myself with finding food. I walked along the riverbank, watching the blackbirds scurrying through the fronds of grass on the ground, and the egrets circling overhead in great swooping arcs of white. It was a beautiful day, and the sun glinted through the leaves of the trees, casting its glow over the land as I sat warming myself.

Summer ended and my belly swelled as I continued to forage for food. There were fewer people visiting the park now, which meant less discarded scraps, and I knew I wasn't eating enough. My paws scuffed the ground, and my legs were stiff as I struggled to make it up and down the bank by the river to drink. I shook my head, trying to clear the fog that had crawled inside my brain as I stumbled around, clumsy and fumbling. I tried to keep going, knowing the time would soon arrive for my pups to be born, but I grew weaker, until one day I collapsed beside a drainage channel.

Crawling inside out of view, I curled up, whimpering to myself as my pups slid out of me onto the concrete floor. I huddled around them, willing them to move and start suckling me. They looked so small and weak as I feverishly nudged one. It didn't respond. I touched the others, pushing them with my nose. Four pups, all dead. I licked each one with a soft caress, nuzzling them and whispering, *I'm sorry,* over each limp body.

Darkness descended outside. I shivered and my legs trembled as I tipped my head low and wrapped myself around my lifeless pups.

CHAPTER EIGHT

I have no idea how long I stayed there in the darkness. The hours and days all merged into one. Eventually, the sun came up one morning, and I dragged myself out of the drainage channel. I didn't know what to do with my pups, now lying stiff on the damp ground. I shivered, not wanting to go back inside that dark place again. With a last glance behind me, I walked away, not caring where my paws took me.

I stumbled out onto the road and started walking towards the next village, wanting to move far away from the car park and my babies. Every time I closed my eyes, I could see them lying there on the concrete floor, eyes closed, huddled together. My feet dragged along the ground as I forced myself to take one step after another.

I kept to the side of the road, oblivious to the cars whizzing past me. My legs were heavy as I lurched along, swaying from side to side, and reeling from the pain inside me. I was so hungry. My head dropped, and I wanted to stop and curl up into a ball and die along with my pups, but something kept moving me forward.

A car pulled up ahead of me and I glanced up, not caring who it was. A woman got out of the car and walked towards me. She held out her hand and whispered to me, and I let her pat me. I was too tired to be frightened, as she walked back to her car and opened the boot. She beckoned me to come nearer, and I crept up to her as a little dog jumped out of the car and trotted over to me.

The woman handed me some food, and I gulped it down. It was delicious, meaty and moist. She placed a plastic dish on the floor and filled it with water and I sank my head into it, sploshing and slurping as the cool liquid eased my throat. I licked my lips, relishing the morsels of food still stuck to my chops. The little dog sniffed me then jumped back in the car, as the lady closed the boot and stood with her hands on her hips, head tilted to one side.

I scrambled forward and looked at the back seat of the car. I knew I should run away; I didn't know who the lady was, but I longed to lie down and rest, and her food had tasted so good. My legs trembled as I measured the distance in my mind. I wasn't sure if I could make it, but I took a deep breath and launched myself upwards. I landed in a heap beside the other dog and quickly lowered my head, not looking at her. *If she growls, I'll jump back down.* But she didn't seem bothered at all and curled up, closing her eyes.

The lady chuckled. "Well, it looks like I've adopted another dog then," she said, and picked up a rug from the footwell. She wrapped it around me, and I rested my head on my paws. The lady walked to the driver's door and got in, looking over her shoulder at me.

"Well, little one, I guess you're coming with me." She started the engine, and I shot up as the car moved, my legs wobbling as I tried to balance. I'd never been in a moving car before.

"It's okay, don't worry, it can't hurt you," she said, as the car picked up speed and I peeked out of the window as the fields and sky raced past me.

I closed my eyes, trying to block it all out. My first time in a car and it was so scary. The noise of the engine was deafening and I could hear the tyres as they rolled along the ground. We turned a corner, and I panicked and sat upright again as everything moved underneath me. The little dog beside me was fast asleep. *Well, she doesn't seem bothered. She's obviously travelled like this before. Maybe it will be alright.*

But I kept my eyes open, just in case, until we pulled up outside the entrance to a farmhouse.

Fear crept into my heart; a red-hot match that flickered, then burst into flames. The heat raced across my back. *What if we've returned to my old place and the farmer that tied me up?* I looked out and drew a long, deep breath through my nose. No, this was a very different farm, brightly painted, with flowers all along the path.

I jumped down and followed the little dog, as the lady called to her. "Come on Cheeky, let's go inside and bring your new friend with you." She rang the doorbell, and a smiling younger woman opened the door.

"Ginie, how lovely to see you again. And Cheeky too. And who's this then? Another waif and stray?"

"Ah yes, well, I was driving here, and I saw this little scrap beside the road. She'd obviously been abandoned and looked hungry, so I stopped. I meant to just give her some food and check if she was alright, but she had other ideas and jumped into my car. So here she is."

They both came over to me. I dropped my head lower, then rolled over and lay on my back. I tried to remember the names of my new friends, Ginie and Cheeky.

"She's a dear little thing, isn't she? But so skinny."

"Yes, she guzzled up the food and water I gave her. I bet she's been on the streets for a long while. All her ribs are showing and her coat is in a dreadful state." Ginie stroked me gently, and I settled down, cherishing each touch, and shivering slightly.

"Well, we'd better feed her up then, hadn't we?" The other lady smiled at me and walked into the kitchen. I followed her, smelling the food before she had even put the bowl on the floor. She placed a separate bowl down for Cheeky, and I waited for Ginie's dog to eat first, not wanting to upset her. I sank my teeth into the food and gobbled it up, my belly contracting and shivering as each mouthful descended. I drank from a bowl of water then followed Cheeky outside and lay down in the yard, licking my paws and savouring the last remnants of food in my whiskers.

That evening, we all went for a walk, following a lane that led to an enormous field. My legs buckled under me with the effort of trying to keep up, as little Cheeky raced ahead. Ginie and her friend talked and laughed together the entire walk. By the time we returned to the farm, my body ached, and it was all I could do to eat some more food before I collapsed.

Ginie placed a blanket on an old chair in the kitchen and lifted me up, placing me onto the seat and wrapping the soft cover around me. I was asleep in minutes, drifting off to the sound of a clock ticking in the background.

The next morning, I woke early and stretched, my muscles shuddering. All was quiet. My first night sleeping inside a house. Out on the road I had slept fitfully, waking every time I heard a noise. Even a leaf falling on my head would startle me, and I often dreamt something was attacking me in my sleep. Every night I tried to find a spot where I could settle with my back against a wall or tree. And before that, I had to stay awake to guard the chickens each night. I sneaked odd naps during the day when the farmer was busy, but there was always Bruno to keep an eye out for. It was amazing being able to sleep all night without being disturbed or frightened.

Ginie, with Cheeky at her feet, came into the kitchen and opened the back door. I stepped outside, sniffing the fresh morning air, and followed Cheeky over to a rough patch of grass.

We returned inside to find fresh bowls of food and water on the floor, and I dived in, scoffing my food in six quick gulps.

"You'll have to learn to eat more slowly, young lady," Ginie said, as I sat beside my chair, waiting for her to lift me up again. It was too high for me to reach; my legs were not strong enough to push me up off the ground. I had no idea where my burst of energy had come from to jump up into her car yesterday, but it had been worth it. Now all I had to do was see what happened next, but I had a good feeling about Ginie and I knew she wouldn't hurt me.

CHAPTER NINE

I slept for hours in the chair that day and woke to find my teats had swollen and were leaking. As I licked them, a desperate sadness descended over me as I remembered my pups. I whimpered as I pictured them lying there, four silent tiny corpses in the corner of the drain. The putrid, dank smell of death was etched in my brain.

Ginie and the other lady were sitting at the kitchen table. I could only hear snippets of their conversation, but I knew they were talking about me.

"If she's lactating now, that means she must have had pups recently."

"Yes, I'm guessing it's because she's eating proper food now. There was certainly no sign of that yesterday. What are we going to do?"

"Well, I ought to take her back to where I found her. See if she leads me to her pups. I'd hate to think they were lying on their own somewhere."

"It seems odd though, doesn't it? A mother wouldn't normally leave her litter alone. She must have been desperate, poor thing."

"Right, well, I'd better get going then. I'll take Cheeky with me in the car to keep her company. I shouldn't be too long."

Ginie lifted me off the chair and fitted a new collar around my neck and behind my shoulders, throwing my old tattered one in the bin. The new one was soft against my skin and I let her attach a lead and walk me out to the car. She lifted me inside and Cheeky settled down beside me. She hadn't really communicated much with me. I got the distinct impression she knew she was Ginie's top dog and probably not too impressed to find me tagging along, but she wasn't nasty to me.

We drove off, and I looked out of the window, but the fields whizzed past me so fast they were a blur of green and brown. I put my head down and tried to close my eyes and ignore what was happening. Suddenly we stopped and Ginie got out, came round, and opened the back door. I peered out and recognised the lane she had found me in. *Oh no, is she getting rid of me?*

I tried to squirm further into the seat. *I don't want to go back out there again on my own. Can't I stay with you?* I wished I could tell her how I felt. My body shook as I lifted a paw towards her.

"You're certainly not in a hurry to find your pups, are you?" she said to me.

She stroked me as I lay there, her hand firm but soothing. I shuddered as I realised what she was asking me. *How can I explain my babies are all dead, and the drainage channel is the last place on earth I would ever want to return to? That dreadful dark hole where my little ones lay still and cold?* I turned around on the seat to face away from the door and huddled closer to Cheeky.

Ginie got back in the car and started the engine. "Okay, little one. I guess there aren't any pups. I'm sure you'd have shown me if there were. Let's go back, shall we?"

I fell asleep. In my dreams, I was in the drainage channel, my babies trapped behind a solid wall. I scrabbled with my claws, trying to break down the concrete but couldn't get through, as their cries grew ever weaker.

I woke yelping, and looked over at Cheeky, expecting her to be laughing at me, but she stretched out a paw and touched me gently. I whimpered, tucking my head around my body, and tried to sleep.

We returned to the farm, and I climbed out of the car. The late afternoon sun warmed my body as I rolled and rolled on the grass. I kicked my legs up in the air as I flipped onto my back, wriggling from side to side, then jumped up and shook myself. *So this is what it feels like to be safe.*

Ginie and her friend were talking.

"What are you going to do with her?"

"Well, the first thing I need to do is give her a bath. She's covered in ticks and fleas. I think I've got some shampoo in the car. Occupational hazard." Ginie smiled.

The other lady laughed. "How is the rescue centre these days?"

"Oh, as busy as ever. I have far too many dogs that need a new home, but I can never resist helping when I find one in distress. It looks like I've added another one to the list."

"Yes, but she is a sweetie. Even though she's in such a mess, she's a proper lady. You can see that."

"I agree. I just wasn't expecting to rescue another dog on this trip. I can't remember the last time I had a holiday. Oh well, there's nothing else for it. I can't leave her now. The vet's closed as it's the weekend, and I have to drive home tomorrow. I'll have to sort things out when I get back to Portugal."

"She won't be missed, that's for sure. Looking at the state of her and her coat, she must have been living wild for a long time. I've certainly never seen her before, and no-one I know round here is missing a dog."

Ginie fetched something from her car, then called me over to a hosepipe attached to the wall. I sat down, remembering with dread how the farmer used to blast me with water if I was dirty. I bowed my head and felt Ginie's hand caressing me as the water trickled over me. She lathered me up with soap that smelt like a pine forest, then washed it all off and towelled me dry. She combed through my fur, gently removing the burrs and tangles. I was clean again and my skin stopped itching almost straight away.

"That will have to do for now," Ginie said to her friend. "Poor girl, I could see all her ribs once she was wet through. But she didn't even murmur. She has a lovely temperament."

"What are you going to call her?"

"I think I'll name her Olalya. It reminds me of the name of your little Spanish village." Ginie ruffled the curls on the top of my head as I lay contented at her feet.

The evening followed the same pattern as the previous day: a walk, food, then bedtime. I curled up on the chair and didn't wake up once until the following morning. After breakfast, Ginie packed her things into bags, walking back and forth out to her car, and I wondered what was happening. *Is she leaving? Will she take me with her or abandon me here?*

I dropped my head and waited.

"Come on. You're coming with me. You can find out what it's like to live in Portugal instead."

I didn't know what Portugal was, but I heard the kindness in her voice and knew it was going to be alright. She loaded up the car, Cheeky jumped inside and Ginie lifted me in beside her. She hooked me up to something on the seat and I turned around, trying to see what it was.

"It's okay, I just need to clip you in. We have a long drive ahead of us and I don't want the police to stop and fine me. So settle down, girl, and we'll get going."

Cheeky seemed unperturbed and so I curled up and tried to sleep as Ginie waved goodbye to her friend and drove away from the farm.

The journey took forever. We stopped twice so Ginie could have a break and we could stretch and walk around and do our business. My head was spinning, and my paws were sweating and clammy. I hardly ate or drank anything. Finally, as night fell, we pulled up beside a row of big metal gates and Ginie jumped out to open them. We drove through one set. She stopped again, shut those gates and opened another set ahead. We drove through those. Then she parked up and shut the second set of gates behind her. *Where are we? Am I trapped in here?*

I could hear dogs barking and howling. There seemed to be hundreds of them. Their voices got louder and louder as I shrank back in the seat, fearful of what was outside the car. Cheeky was looking out of the window, wagging her tail, and I stared at her in astonishment. She wasn't frightened at all, and as soon as Ginie had opened the door and unhooked her, she shot out of the car and raced off.

Ginie reached over and unhooked me and I waited as she came round, then gently picked me up and set me down on the ground. In front of me was an enormous garden and several buildings. *But where are all the dogs?* I could hear them barking and yowling, but apart from Cheeky racing around, there were no other dogs to be seen.

"Come on, Olalya. You can meet them all tomorrow. Come inside here with me and we'll get you settled down for the night."

I went for a wee, then followed Ginie into a large building, blinking as she switched on a big fluorescent light overhead. It was a kitchen with a wooden table in the centre and lots of white cupboards along the walls. She gave me some food and water and I gulped it down, then settled myself on a rug on the floor.

Ginie went outside, and a rush of noise and barking flooded in from the garden. My heart fluttered. I took a deep breath. *It's okay. It's safe in here.* I tried to count how many dogs were out there, but gave up. There were too many unfamiliar noises all tumbling over each other, with lots of howling and whining, feet pattering, and bowls clattering.

I fell into an uneasy sleep. I didn't know what was outside or where I was, and no idea what morning would bring.

CHAPTER TEN

The next morning, the same roar of noise assaulted my senses. I peered out of the window. *How many dogs does she have?* Outside was a jumbled mass of fur and paws, heads bobbing, bodies racing around as Ginie released more and more dogs from a concrete building in the garden.

I hid in the corner as Ginie came into the kitchen. The barking and noise increased as she opened the door, then faded again as the door slammed shut behind her. The other dogs were still in the garden, but Cheeky had trotted inside.

Ginie turned on the tap over the sink. A high-pitched squeal came from the pipework above my head and I shot up in the air, my heart thumping. Everything was making me nervous.

"Come on, Olalya. We're off to the vet's to get you checked out, and the groomers to sort out that fur of yours." She hooked a lead onto my collar and walked towards the door. I hung back, not wanting to meet all those dogs.

"Don't worry, they won't hurt you. Let's go."

My head was spinning, but most of the dogs were busy playing together and hardly noticed me as we walked to Ginie's car. Cheeky jumped inside onto the back seat, and Ginie lifted me up beside her. All I could hear as we drove away were the dogs barking and howling.

We stopped in front of a concrete and glass building, and Ginie led me inside. We walked into a small room that smelt of lemons. A man wearing a white coat followed us into the room. Ginie picked me up and set me on a metal table in the centre, and I stood perched on the shiny surface. She stroked me as the man looked at me. *You must be the vet.* I didn't trust him yet, even though it was obvious Ginie liked him.

"Let me guess, another rescue?" He laughed at Ginie, as she nodded her head.

"Yes, I know. And on my weekend off as well. This one's from Spain though. Can you check in case she has been chipped, although I doubt she has?"

The vet waved something around my neck and body, then shook his head. "No, no chip. Not a surprise though, looking at her." He ran his hand along my back and checked my eyes and teeth. "She's in a real state, isn't she? You can feel her ribs even through this matted fur. That will all have to come off."

"I know. Next stop is the groomer." Ginie stroked me and patted my head. "I think she just needs feeding up, though. There's nothing else wrong with her?"

"No, she'll be fine once she has gained some weight. I'll schedule her in to be sterilised at the end of next week, if you like. Give her a few days to get used to everything first and fatten up a bit."

"Yes, that's great. And she'll need all her jabs. And a passport. The usual things before I can arrange for her to be adopted. But she's a special girl. I won't let just anyone take her. I've grown rather fond of her already."

"She's had several litters. And not easy ones either, looking at her. I'm sure she'll be glad not to have any more. I'm not sure how she survived the last round." He touched my head. "You know she's only recently given birth? I take it you didn't find any pups with her?"

"Yes, we guessed that, and I took her back to where I found her. There was no reaction. Nothing. She wanted to stay in the car."

"That figures. She's so underweight and emaciated. There's no way she'd have carried to full term. They would have been stillborn."

The vet patted me, and I bent my head as I listened to him. I knew he was talking about my pups, and I felt their loss as keenly as if it had only just happened.

"She's a Spanish water dog. Maybe with a bit of poodle thrown in. It's hard to tell. But definitely a water dog. The Spanish version is different from the Portuguese water dog. They are farm dogs, and many have never even seen more than a puddle of water or a river. She's got webbed feet. Look. Only at the front, though, unusually."

He lifted me down and placed me on a metal plate on the floor. "As I thought. Well underweight. She's only eleven kilos. Almost half the weight she should be. I'd aim for about eighteen kilos if you can. She'll be a wonderful dog. She's got a lovely face."

Ginie thanked him and we left, walking down the road to a house tucked away behind a large sign. "Come on, let's get that fur sorted."

She led me inside and before I knew it; I was standing on top of another table and a lady was trimming all my curls away. I stood still, glad to be rid of my matted fur. She was very gentle with me; it wasn't at all like when the farmer attacked me with his clippers. I shivered as I recalled how rough he had been. Soon I felt light and free, all my black curls lying in a heap on the table. The air was cool and fresh as it furled across my bare skin. The lady lifted me up and placed me in a big sink. Another bath. This time, the foam smelt like flowers. I shook my head as the bubbles splashed into my ears and eyes.

"You can see all her ribs now, poor girl." The lady talked to Ginie as she towelled me dry. "And look at all these marks on her back and hind legs. She must have been beaten. Terrible."

"I'll never understand how someone can hit a dog. She's had a hard time of it, that's for sure. At least now I can find her a special home. She deserves it." Ginie thanked her, and we walked out to the car, where Cheeky was sitting waiting for us.

We returned to Ginie's place, and the dogs started crying and howling as soon as she parked up. Ginie lifted me down, and I waited for the onslaught. Several big dogs raced over to sniff me and say hello as I stood awkward and confused, not knowing what to do. I thought they were going to knock me over as more and more dogs bounded up to me, pushing and sniffing. I retreated, head down, and waited for the inevitable. A rush of air swirled around me as they all backed away, giving me space again. I breathed out. *That wasn't too bad. At least they didn't hurt me or try to mount me.*

Ginie placed me onto an old table and took some photos of me. I looked away, my face tingling. *Why is she taking my picture? All my fur has gone. I'm almost naked and so skinny.* Then I shook myself and held my head high as I remembered everything I had been through. *I'm still here and I have survived everything. Maybe things will get better for me now.*

I found a quiet corner and tried to settle down. A couple of older dogs came over and sat with me, and I relaxed a little. The next few days were a mixture of time spent in the garden with all the other dogs, and nights spent sleeping on my own in the kitchen area.

I wasn't sure if this was to be my new home or not. *Is Ginie going to keep me? Will I have to stay here with all these other dogs? And sleep in the kennel area at night with the others?* I didn't fancy that very much; it was so noisy and there were too many boisterous dogs in there.

One morning, Ginie took me out in the car. She parked outside the same building and took me in to see the vet man again. She said, "I'll pick you up later," and walked out, leaving me behind. I didn't know what was happening and I couldn't stop my legs from shaking.

"Don't worry, I won't hurt you. You won't feel anything." The vet cradled me in his arms as he lifted me up onto the table.

A sharp sting in my shoulder. Then everything went dark. When I woke up, I had a strange plastic cone wrapped around my neck. I twisted my head, but the vet had fixed the cone to my collar. My stomach was sore. I tried to reach around to lick myself, but the cone was in the way. I fell back asleep. When I stirred again, Ginie was there, and she picked me up and took me home, placing me on a rug in the kitchen beside a bowl of food and water.

I stayed there for several days, only venturing out to do my business, as I clattered into the walls and bushes outside. The cone made everything more difficult, and I hoped it wasn't a permanent thing. I could eat and drink, but curling up to sleep was difficult, and I so wanted to lick myself where I hurt but couldn't reach.

Then came the morning when Ginie took the cone away. I shook myself, thrilled to be free again.

"Today's a busy day for you, Olalya. You're going to meet two people I think you are going to like. If they like you, they might adopt you. Let's get you looking your best, shall we?"

I didn't know what she meant, as I stood there and let her fuss me. *Why am I meeting more people? Am I going to live somewhere else? What if she doesn't actually mean that? Is it a trick? What if the farmer has tracked me down and is coming to get me? Surely Ginie wouldn't let that happen?*

I lay down on my blanket and stared at the door, waiting, my mind racing with dark thoughts.

CHAPTER ELEVEN

The door opened and Ginie strolled in, followed by a lady and a man. I breathed a sigh of relief; it wasn't the farmer. The lady stretched out her hand and whispered, "Hello."

She looked at me so tenderly my heart soared. I gazed into her eyes and saw such love there that I almost fell backwards. I was confused; it was as if I already knew her, and yet I had never seen her before. I snuffled her hand as she stroked the top of my head. Her touch was gentle yet reassuring, and I sat beside her, knowing instinctively that I was safe.

The man with her smiled and said, "Hello little one." I walked over to him, letting him pat my head as I stood near his legs. But it was the lady that drew me back to her side. I longed to feel her touch and listen to her voice whispering to me. I settled down beside her, her hand caressing me as she talked to Ginie. A surge of warmth rose inside me. *Is this really happening?* I knew straight away I wanted to be with her; that somehow, we were meant to be together.

They stayed for a while, asking lots of questions, then stood up to leave. I jumped up, startled. *Where are they going?* Ginie motioned to me, and I followed the couple outside. They said goodbye, climbed into their car and drove down the path. I ran behind the car as it reached first one set of gates, then the other. The lady looked back at me in the mirror as the car sped away.

My legs were like concrete as I plodded back into the kitchen. Ginie gave me some biscuits, then left me as I lay down and tried to sleep. *Where have they gone? Why couldn't I have left with them? Didn't they like me? Wasn't that why they had come today, to see if they liked me?* I thought about the lady and how I had felt when she stroked me, and my heart sank. *What if I never see her again?*

The next day I sat all morning by the gates hoping she would return, and I did the same the following day. Nothing. Life carried on as normal. The dogs all raced around, some stretched out in the sunshine, others playing a mad game of chase round and round the paths, and I tried to forget about what had happened. *Perhaps I have to stay with Ginie forever. Well, at least no-one hits me here and I get fed every day. It could be a lot worse.* But there was something inside me that whispered there was more to life. And that somehow it was connected to that lady.

The third day was sunny as I sat outside in the corner, still watching each time the gates opened, hoping. Before I even heard a vehicle approaching, I knew she was nearby. Their silver car came through the gates, and I stood up to meet it. The door opened, and it was her. She had returned. My heart was pounding. The man stepped out too, and they walked over towards me.

I raced up to the lady and fell into her arms as she knelt down.

"I'm back, my little one. And you're coming home with us today."

I nuzzled into her, listening to her soft words, and a warm surge of love burst inside me. *She came back for me. Everything is going to be alright.*

We walked into the kitchen, and they chatted to Ginie, the lady stroking me the whole time. They sorted out lots of paperwork and I found out their names as they sat talking. Alyson and Dave. They were to be my new parents.

I trotted over to Ginie and licked her hand. I needed to tell her how thankful I was she had stopped her car that day and let me jump in.

She stooped down and hugged me. "You're going to have a wonderful life. Be a good girl for me, Olalya. I will miss you. You're a very special little dog, and I'll never forget you."

"You can come and see her anytime," Alyson said, as she gathered up the papers on the table and picked up my lead. "We'll go to the pet shop on the way home and buy her some things, including a new collar and lead. I'll drop these old ones back to you next week."

With that, we stepped outside into the sunshine, and Alyson hugged Ginie. "Thank you so much. The minute I saw that photo of her online, I knew she was the one for us. We'll love her and take good care of her, don't worry."

"I know you will. Have a wonderful life, Olalya."

Alyson picked me up and placed me onto the backseat of their car on a fluffy rug. She clipped me in and stroked my head. "We've got a long ride now, sweetheart. But I'll be here in the front, and you'll be fine. We're taking you home with us."

I didn't want to look out of the window at everything that was rushing by, so I curled up and tucked my head around my body. We stopped in front of a shop and Alyson jumped out, but Dave stayed with me, reaching over to pat me and talk to me, and I relaxed again. Soon Alyson was back, a big grin on her face as she settled into her seat.

"I got lots of new things for our girl," she said, as Dave laughed.

"I bet you bought half the store. She's worth it though, dear little thing. She's such a beauty."

The journey seemed to last ages, but it was all straight roads, and I was feeling fine, until suddenly we came to a big roundabout. My stomach heaved as I shot up. I couldn't stop myself and threw up all over the rug. My legs shook as I dipped my head, expecting to be told off. A rush of heat spread across my body as I cringed, anxious about what would happen next. I hardly knew these people. *What if they are angry? Or return me to Ginie?*

I needn't have worried. Alyson stretched out her hand to touch me. "It's okay, little one. We went round that one too fast for you, eh?" She turned to Dave. "We'd better slow down on the bends. I'm not sure she's used to being in a car and it all got a bit much for her, poor thing."

She reached behind and folded the blanket over the pile of vomit. "There, it'll be alright. Not much further now, and we'll be home."

I couldn't believe it. I wasn't in trouble. I settled down, closing my eyes to stop the world from spinning past the windows, and tried to calm myself. My heart was racing, though. *Home.* It sounded such a pleasant word. I wondered what it would be like. *Where do they live? In a house or on a farm? Will I sleep outside? What if they're like the farmer? Will I have to stay outside and guard chickens again? What if they already have a dog? What if the other dog doesn't like me? Or if they have a dog like Bruno?*

I had so many questions racing around my head, and I barely realised I had fallen asleep until we pulled up opposite a house and Alyson said, "We're home."

I looked out of the window, suddenly fearful of what awaited me. Alyson seemed to sense my reticence as she opened the door and set me down on the pavement. "Shall we go for a quick walk first? I'm sure you must be bursting after that long journey? Then we'll show you inside."

I found a patch of grass for a wee, then turned around. I took a deep breath as we reached the house and I walked up the path. My new life was about to begin.

CHAPTER TWELVE

Dave opened the front door, but I hung back, unsure of what to do.

"Come on, Missy, you can follow us inside. This is your home too now. Have a good look around."

I walked in slowly, sniffing the air. Two large sofas and a squishy chair. *I wonder if they'll let me sit on one of those?* They looked very cosy. A room on the left had an enormous bed inside. Next to that was a room that smelt different, like flowers after the rain has soaked them.

"That's the bathroom, then next to that is our office." Alyson described each room, and I relaxed a little. Next was a staircase that reached up high. I hadn't climbed up or down steps before and wasn't sure about them. Then suddenly I stopped dead and my heart started pounding. There were more steps going down into a deep well of black. I balked at the sight of them. *Where do they go? Why are they there? Do I have to go down them?*

Instantly, I was back in the drainage channel with my pups beside me. The darkness overwhelmed me like a heavy sheet of plastic wrapped around my head, leeching the air. I panted, unable to breathe, and shook my head from side to side, trying to shake away the memories.

"What's up baby?" Alyson knelt beside me, talking to me in her soft voice. "Oh, I think it's the stairs," she said to Dave. "The light's not on, and it must look scary."

She flicked a switch on the wall. Instantly, the area flooded with light, and I crept over and peeped down. It didn't seem so bad, just steps that disappeared round a corner, but I still didn't want to go down there.

"Next up is the kitchen," Alyson said, walking into a bright room. "And this is your bed, and here are your bowls."

I sidled past the steps and into the kitchen and looked around, smelling the air. This room was better. It had nice big windows and lots of light and another door at the end. My bed was a big plastic shell with a fleece blanket inside. There were lots of small fluffy things already perched in there. I didn't know what they were and decided to ignore them.

I went over to look at a shiny door. A dog was staring at me, and I shot backwards, lowering my head. *Is there another dog in here? Where did he come from? Why can't I smell him?* I cowered down, not knowing what else to do.

"Oh gosh, look. She's just seen a reflection of herself in the oven door." Dave chuckled as Alyson walked over and knelt beside me.

"Everything's okay. It's just a mirror. There's only a picture of you in there. It can't hurt you." I peered over and saw the dog again and Alyson crouched beside it. *Is that what I look like?*

"And out here is the back garden. Come and explore with me."

I walked over to the door. There was another set of steps, and I hung back, my paws skidding on the tiled floor.

"Have you never been down steps before?" Alyson said. "Never mind. We'll soon get you used to them. I tell you what, why don't I pick you up and carry you today? Then you can have a nosey around the garden."

Her arms reached under my tummy as she lifted me and carried me down the steps, dropping me gently onto the ground at the bottom. I took a big, deep breath of fresh air and wagged my tail.

The garden was mostly concrete, but it was big, and the blue sky was enormous above us. I trotted over to what I thought was a strip of grass, then stopped and inhaled. It was weird. It looked like grass, but it smelt of chemicals and plastic. I sniffed it again and wrinkled my nose.

"It's fake grass." Alyson laughed as she ran her hand over it.

I stepped forward. My paws sank into the surface, the blades tickling my pads as I walked. I'd never seen anything like it before.

I circled round all four edges of the garden, climbed up a steep slope, and realised I was back at the front door of the house. Satisfied, I walked inside and made my way to the kitchen. I shuddered. *I have to pass those steps again.* Taking a deep breath, I scurried past them, not looking down. My heart was racing.

I lay down on my bed, closing my eyes for a second, then opened them again quickly, unsure of whether it was alright for me to go to sleep or not.

Alyson patted my head gently. "You have a snooze. You look worn out. We can go out later." My eyes were closed almost before she had finished speaking.

Waking up, I stretched and looked around the room. Everything was still the same. The house was quiet. I padded out of the kitchen, my paws tapping on the tiled floor, wondering where everyone was. I found Alyson in the office. She jumped off the chair she was sitting on and came over to me.

"There you are. I've been waiting for you to wake up. Shall we go for a walk now? I'll show you where we live." She picked up some things from the table.

"I've got a new collar for you. Here you go." She unhooked the one Ginie had given me and slipped it off, replacing it with a harness that went round my neck and under my front legs and belly. She altered the straps and made sure it fitted, then stepped back.

"There, now you have a nice new collar. And everyone will know you are ours." She attached a lead. It hooked on across my back rather than around my neck. It fitted well and felt secure. I trotted outside beside her, the lead hanging loosely between us.

We walked along the road past lots of houses and turned down into an open space. I stopped and looked ahead, sniffing madly. Far in the distance, water sparkled and there was a salty tang in the air. I spotted the perfect stretch of grass and Alyson praised me after I had done my business. Then she picked it up in a plastic bag and carried it to a nearby bin. *How odd. I wonder why she's done that?*

There were so many new things to investigate, and I soon grew tired. My legs were stiff and sore and I wanted to rest.

We walked slowly home, and Alyson led me into the kitchen, where she laid down a bowl full of food on the floor. It smelt fabulous, rich and meaty, as I dived in and devoured it all. I licked my face, wanting to make sure I had eaten every single bit, then sat back on my bed. I cleaned my paws, let out a long, satisfying sigh, and fell into a deep sleep.

It was dark outside when I woke up and I looked around for a moment, unsure of where I was. Alyson and Dave were in the kitchen and they both smiled at me.

"Time for your night-time walk," Alyson said and picked up my lead. I was glad. I needed to go for a wee, but didn't know how to ask to go outside. A quick walk along the road and I found a patch of grass. *Phew.* We walked home, and Dave handed me a biscuit, which I gobbled up.

"Right, time for bed now, little lady. You can sleep in here. Don't worry about anything. We'll see you in the morning, and I'll take you for a nice walk again." Alyson sat on the floor beside my bed in the kitchen, rubbing my head with long, soft strokes. My eyelids were heavy, and I struggled to stay awake. It had been a very long and busy day. There was so much to remember.

Her voice was soft as she caressed me, soothing me as I lay there. I had never known so much love before, or felt so safe, as I dropped my head onto my paws and fell asleep.

CHAPTER THIRTEEN

The next morning, I woke early. Alyson was already in the kitchen, dressed and holding my lead.

"Want to go for a walk, little one?" I stretched and stood up as she clipped my lead on and led me outside. The air was crisp, as the first rays of sunlight inched across the sky.

We crossed the road and turned into a small lane bordered by grass and plants on either side. In the middle was a big hollow, full of little paths and boulders, and it smelt wonderful. I could sense there were rabbits there, and the birds were singing and chirruping in the trees. I trotted along, stopping to sniff everything as Alyson laughed at me and unclipped my lead.

"There you go. Now you can snuffle away to your heart's content. Just stay close to me."

I thought she might drag me along at a fast pace, but I needn't have worried. I could stop and take everything in and learn about this new place in my own time. The lane looped round in a big semi-circle, and there were intriguing paths leading off in all directions. There was a lot to explore.

Alyson seemed to enjoy the walk too, as she patted me on the head and smiled. "We're going to have such fun together. We'll build your strength up slowly, then we can go on longer walks each day. It'll just be you and me every morning like this."

She clipped on my lead when we returned to the main road, and we walked home. Alyson placed a fresh bowl of water down on the floor in the kitchen and I drank eagerly, tired from the walk. Then came a lovely big bowl of food, which disappeared very quickly! Dave wandered into the kitchen and chatted to Alyson as I lay on my bed, licking my paws clean.

I thought about what had happened to me in the last few days. I liked them both. *But what if I get settled? Then they move away like that family did and leave me behind?* I had felt comfortable once before, with that nice old lady, until the man had showed up and shooed me away. *Don't get too excited. Not yet.*

They went into the office. I walked in behind them, my back beside the wall. *Am I allowed in here? Should I have stayed on my bed?* Alyson beckoned me over.

"Hello Missy. Do you want to join us?" She stood up and walked over to me. "I think I'll bring her bed in here. Perhaps we should buy another bed and leave it in the office so that she knows where she can sit?"

"You'll end up buying a bed for every room, you softie," Dave replied, laughing. "Maybe we can get one of those big cushions they do for dogs?"

"That's a great idea. I'll go shopping later."

I fell asleep. My legs were sore, and the walk had taken a lot out of me that morning. The next thing I knew it was lunchtime, and Alyson took me for a quick walk. I understood she wanted me to do my business each time we went out, and I was happy to oblige. She praised me, and we strolled home.

So far, I had seen no other dogs, although sometimes I heard barking in the distance. I scampered down the slope into the back garden and spotted a tiny old dog in the garden next door. I walked up to the fence and sniffed, trying to say hello. The dog peered over at me and bowed her head.

"She sleeps outside, so you'll see lots of her." Alyson said. "But she's old now. I'm not sure she can see or hear too well anymore."

After lunch, Dave said to Alyson, "Why don't we take our girl to the beach? And we'll have to decide on a name for her soon. We can't keep calling her 'little one' or Missy forever."

"Yes, that's true. I can't decide though. Every time I think of a name, it doesn't seem to suit her."

"Well, what about something different? You know me and my *Monty Python* sense of humour. I've always wanted a dog called cat."

Alyson raised her eyes upwards and tutted. "Trust you to think of a daft name like that." She waved her finger at him. "Although... what if we spelled it K-a-t? With a k, not a c?" She nodded her head. "Yes, that would work. It's certainly unusual."

"What do you reckon, Missy?" Dave said. "Do you like the name Kat?"

I wagged my tail. It didn't bother me what they called me, but I knew being given a name was an important moment. That meant they liked me enough to want to keep me, and I wagged my tail again and looked up, panting.

"There you are. She likes it. So... Kat the dog she is."

Alyson grinned. "Right. Let's take Kat out and introduce her to the beach." She led me outside, and we strolled over to their car parked in a space on the other side of the road. She opened the rear passenger door, and I hung back, waiting.

"You're still not strong enough in those legs, are you?" She lifted me up and placed me on the back seat, clipping me in. "Don't worry, we'll soon build you up with all the nice food we're giving you. You'll be jumping in here on your own in no time."

Dave drove through the village, and I stared out of the window, taking everything in. We parked up, and I tried to climb down when Alyson opened the door, as she hooked my lead on.

"Okay, let's go," she said, laughing as I pulled on the lead, eager to discover where we were. I sniffed the air. It smelt different, salty and fresh, as I strained forward.

"The main beach is pretty busy, and it's high tide," Dave said. "Why don't we walk along the lane beside the river beach today? It'll be quieter."

We set off on a sandy path, lined with dunes and grasses. I was so excited. It was all new to me, and I kept pausing to sniff everything.

"Do you think she'll be okay off her lead here?" Dave asked.

"Well, she was fine this morning round the lane without a lead. Let's give it a try, shall we?" Alyson unhooked me and I trotted off in front of them, happy to be free.

I stopped to sniff a plant, then suddenly a whooshing sound spun above my head. A giant white bird swooped low, so close I could see its beady eye and crooked yellow beak. Its wings beat a rhythmic throb as it rushed past me. I was instantly back at the farm in my mind, remembering the crows whirling and squawking as the farmer snatched my mother from me.

I bent my head down. *Go away, leave me alone.* The bird swept round in a circle above me, and I panicked and ran, desperate to get away from it. My legs hurt as I pounded down the path, ducking my head low, my eyes squinting into the sun. I raced and raced until I stopped, completely out of breath. The bird was nowhere to be seen. *Good, I'm safe now.*

I glanced behind me and panicked. *Where are Alyson and Dave?* I spun round. There was only wide-open space all around me. I shook my head. *Stop. Think. Where did I run from?* I looked again, more slowly this time. There was a couple walking in the distance. *That must be them.*

I ran in their direction. As I got closer, I realised it wasn't Alyson or Dave. I stopped. My chest was heaving as I started panting. *I'm lost. I've lost them. What do I do now?* I took great gulps of air, my legs shaking as I tried to calm down.

The lady walked over to me and stretched out her hand. I backed away. *You're not Alyson. I want to see her again, not you.*

"It's okay, don't be frightened. Are you lost?"

I looked over at her, then behind me. Someone was shouting and waving their arms in the air. I stood still, not sure what to do.

The person in the distance drew closer. They started running, still waving a hand in the air. It was Alyson. I sank down on the ground and waited. She came racing up, and I could hear her gasping as she got closer.

"There you are. Oh baby, I thought we'd lost you." She reached down and hugged me, then turned to the couple stood nearby.

"Thank goodness you were here. Thank you for helping. We've only had her for a day, and she got spooked by a seagull flying overhead. She ran off scared and we couldn't catch her. She must have seen you and thought it was us."

Dave came running over and dropped to his knees beside me on the ground.

"Well, you probably shouldn't have had her off her lead then," the woman replied, as she sniffed and folded her arms. The man with her shrugged and walked off.

"Yes, well, thank you again anyway," Alyson said and gave me a big kiss on the top of my head. "I'm just glad we caught her."

The woman strode off to catch up with her husband, as I stood up and shook myself.

"Snotty cow," Alyson said, as she attached the lead onto my collar.

"Yes, but she had a point. We probably need to spend more time training Kat before we let her off her lead." Dave dusted his trousers.

"I'll work on that. She'll be alright. I guess we don't know what happened to Kat before, or what her triggers are. That bird spooked her, and she was off. We'll have to watch out for that in the future." Alyson looked down at me and I could see how much she loved me already. I was so worried I'd have been in trouble for running away.

"Yes, I think that would be wise," Dave replied. "Poor thing. Who knows what her life was like before Ginie found her? Never mind, she's with us now and she's going to be fine."

In the car on the way home, I thought about what had happened and what they had said. *If only they knew what my life had been like.* Although I was glad I couldn't tell them about my years on the farm and later trying to survive out on the road once I had escaped. That was a time in my life I just wanted to forget.

CHAPTER FOURTEEN

My mornings settled into a nice routine of waking up and going for a walk first thing with Alyson. We went a little further each day, always coming back to loop around the deserted rabbit lane. I was desperate to spot one, but so far, they had evaded me. My nose twitched and my tail quivered with excitement each time I caught their scent, as I ran, nose to the ground, following each deliciously spicy trail of droppings.

One thing I didn't like were the gaps in the road. They had a metal grill over them and the first time I peered into one; I recoiled backwards. Too many terrible memories came shooting to the surface of my mind whenever I looked down into a deep hole like that. I learnt to avoid them, walking round them carefully. The first time it happened, Alyson watched me but didn't say anything. She patted me on the head to reassure me and we carried on down the road.

Our morning walks were special. It was always quiet. There were very few cars around and we rarely saw anyone else. Alyson liked to go out just as the sun was rising. It was a little cold at first, but I soon warmed up as I trotted along. My legs were getting stronger, and I was less tired. I was keen to go further, there was so much to explore.

One day, I listened to Alyson chatting to Dave.

"I'm not sure what to do when we go out. We'll have to leave her sometimes on her own. What do you think?" I knew she was talking about me.

"Well, she's been great so far. She hasn't done a thing indoors. She's very clean. I was expecting the odd upset on the floor in the kitchen overnight."

"No, she always waits until we are on a walk. We've established a good routine, out first thing with me, then again before lunch. We usually take her out in the afternoon once we've finished working, then there's her quick bedtime piddle walk."

"I'm not sure I want her wandering round the entire house when we're out. Why don't I get a stair gate like they sell for toddlers? We could fit it to the kitchen door, then if we go out, Kat can stay in the kitchen with her water bowl and bed. She'd be okay in there."

"That might work. Let's try it and see."

I was confused. *Dave said he was going to fit a gate?* The gate that led to the field at the farm was the only one I could picture. That was a big wooden thing. *Surely Dave wouldn't attach one of those to the kitchen door?* I licked my paws, trying to make sense of it all, as he went out, jangling his car keys.

Alyson took me out for a walk and by the time we returned, Dave was home and there was a new white plastic object fixed across the kitchen door. I sniffed it tentatively; it smelt funny, and I backed away.

"It's alright, it's a gate. Look, this is what we'll do." Dave called me into the kitchen, then closed the plastic gate behind me, clipping it shut with a little lever on the top. It had vertical bars, but I could see through the gaps in them out to the hallway, so it wasn't too bad.

"Let's try going out just for five minutes, then come back. Slowly get her used to us not being here." Dave picked up his keys, and they both walked into the hallway, closing the gate behind them. I hurried over to the gate, watching as Dave stepped outside.

"I'll be back in a minute. Don't worry." Alyson followed Dave, shutting the front door behind her.

There was an echo of the door banging. Then silence. It was eerie.

The clock ticking in the office sounded so loud. I shuddered, my paws clattering on the tiled floor as I padded around, checking the room. *What do I do now? What if they don't return?* I tried to stop panting, but my heart was racing.

Suddenly a key turned in the lock, and the front door swung open, the hallway flooding with sunlight.

"We're back," Alyson said and hurried to the kitchen, opening the gate and enveloping me in a hug. I licked her hand and whirled around, wagging my tail and panting.

"Well, someone looks pleased to see us," Dave said as he strode into the kitchen. He opened my favourite cupboard door, the one with all my food and treats inside, and handed me a biscuit. "Good girl, well done."

"I told you we wouldn't be long." Alyson gave me a second biscuit.

Oh well, if I get biscuits every time, maybe it won't be too bad. I snuggled onto my bed as they made their dinner together. Alyson went to the cupboard under the stairs after they had eaten and picked something up. I was only half awake and didn't see what it was until she started sweeping the floor near me.

I leapt up and whined, shrinking against the wall, trying to get away from her. She was holding a broom, just like the one the farmer used to beat me with. *Surely, she wouldn't hit me, though? She's been so nice to me.* The rational part of my brain tried to reason it all through, but I couldn't help it. I started shaking and whimpered.

"Oh baby, what's wrong?" Alyson set the broom against the wall and came over to me. "Wow, you really don't like that, do you?" The tips of her fingers caressed my head, and I shuddered. "It's okay, little one. No-one's going to hurt you here. Shush. It's alright."

"Poor thing. We really don't know what has happened to her, do we?" Dave came over and put an arm around Alyson, who looked as if she was about to cry.

"I'd never do anything to upset her. I assumed the vacuum cleaner might be a bit much for her, but I never thought the broom would frighten her."

"Well, we know she was beaten, by what Ginie told us. You can see

the scars on her back legs. Maybe someone hit her with a broom."
Dave stroked my head, and I took a deep breath.

"Bless her. How could anyone hurt her? She's such a sweetie."
Alyson tucked the broom away. "Can you distract her so I can finish
up in here?"

"Come on, Kat, you come into the lounge with me. I've got a
surprise for you." Dave walked out, and I followed him. He carried on
talking to Alyson. "I forgot. I bought one of those beds you mentioned
when I was out. It's still in the boot. I'll go and get it."

He went outside to the car. I trotted out and watched from the
drive as he returned carrying an enormous bag. He set it down and
pulled out a huge padded bed, which he put on the floor in the lounge.

"Here you go, try that." He patted it and I walked over and climbed
on top. My body sank into the comfy cushion. It was spongy and
fluffy. *Wonderful.*

"Your new bed." Alyson sat on the floor beside me, stroking me as I
closed my eyes. *Everything is going to be alright.*

After that, they went out sometimes, leaving me in the kitchen with
the gate shut. I was fine once I knew they would always return and
give me a biscuit or two. One day, Alyson left the radio playing,
promising they wouldn't be long. I settled down and tried to sleep, but
when the music ended, loud voices started talking. It was weird, and I
didn't like it very much.

A loud beep came from the hallway. Then everything went quiet.
The radio was no longer playing music. A sharp crack sounded
outside, and I jumped up. I tried to figure out where the noise had
come from. My legs trembled. *I know that sound.* Instantly, I was back
at the farm again. *Will those memories never leave me?*

My body stiffened as a shiver ran through me. *I remember that noise.*
Alyson had been walking beside me early one morning when I had
heard the same sound. A loud, ripping bang that echoed across the
valley, haunting and mysterious.

"That's just a farmer hunting," she had explained. "They're out shooting. It's Sunday. Don't worry. They're probably killing the rabbits, poor things."

Shooting. Killing. So that's what hunting means. The farmer took my mom away, and that was the next sound I heard. The same sharp crack echoing around the farm. And I never saw her again.

Suddenly it all slotted into place, and I trembled. *The farmer had shot my mom because she hadn't protected the chickens. She had grown too old to do her job and so he killed her.*

I shook my head. Memories hurtled through my mind. My mom's startled face as the farmer dragged her away. The gun firing. The crows whirling overhead. Then the silence. I was back there hiding in the shadows, the smell of blood and dead chickens all around me. Red swirls of colour flashed across my eyes, and I ground my teeth, growling as a surge of anger rose inside me.

I stood up, wanting to attack something, anything. I crashed into the vegetable rack, snatched a potato, and threw it into the air. I grabbed another, then another, scattering them on the floor. Then I picked up an onion, but that tasted bitter, so I dropped it, spitting the slimy skin out of my mouth.

He had killed her. Tears pricked my eyes like sharp daggers, stopping me from seeing properly. I staggered over to the fridge, slamming into the bottles of water standing on the floor. I picked one up by the handle, gasping as I lifted it up and heaved it across the room. It landed with a crash as I raced back to grab another one.

I looked up in horror. I had been so busy I hadn't heard Alyson and Dave come home. They were standing by the kitchen door, staring over the gate at me. I dropped the water bottle on the ground and gazed around. There were potatoes, onions and water bottles scattered all over the kitchen floor. I hung my head low, suddenly ashamed of what I had done. *I'm going to be in big trouble now.*

Alyson walked in and set her bag down on the table. "What's happened here then? You have made a mess, haven't you?"

"The electric's gone off. But that wouldn't have spooked her, would it?" Dave asked, flicking switches in a box on the wall in the hallway.

"No, but I left the radio on. Maybe she didn't like that?"

"Well, something has definitely upset her," Dave said, as he came into the kitchen and started picking everything up off the floor.

"I can't believe she managed to lift one of these water bottles and fling it around. They're five litre bottles. And really heavy."

"Oh well, no harm done. We might never know what set her off, poor thing."

"No, very true. We'll give her that one. Chalk it up as a teenage strop." Alyson picked up my lead and waved her finger at me. "But hey, don't do it again, eh? Come on, Missy, let's take you out for a walk, shall we?"

I can't believe it. I'm not in trouble? I walked outside into the bright sunshine and shook myself. I didn't know what I was expecting, but it wasn't that. As we set off on our walk, I vowed never to do anything like that again. Suddenly I realised how lucky I was. I lifted my head up, feeling the warm sun on my face, and smiled. It was time to put the past behind me.

CHAPTER FIFTEEN

"What are we going to say to Ginie? She's expecting us to call her soon about Kat. She's still only here temporarily, remember, until we make it official and adopt her." Alyson was busy loading the dishwasher after breakfast. I always paid attention to this job in case she dropped any food on the floor. She had told me not to lick any of the plates they stacked in there, which seemed a little unfair. I didn't know why they had that machine. I'd do a much better job of cleaning everything if they would let me. I rested my head on my paws. But I kept my eyes glued to the floor. Just in case.

"I'm not sure, to be honest. She seems to have settled in, but she had that fit in the kitchen the other day. Why don't we give it another week or two before we decide? Let's make sure she's happy to be here, and we're certain," said Dave. I pricked my ears up. *That doesn't sound too good.*

"Well, *you* can have more time if you need it. But I made my mind up the moment I saw her. She's our girl, and there's absolutely no way she's going back to Ginie. Ever." Alyson threw the tea towel she was holding down on the worktop and marched out of the room. I looked over at Dave, then trotted out to find Alyson.

"I'm sorry. I'm sure she's going to be fine. It's me, I guess." Dave followed us out to the lounge, where I was sitting on the floor beside Alyson. "I've never had a dog before. It's alright for you. You grew up always having a dog in the house. And you have a natural way with animals. Anyone can see how much Kat adores you already. I need a little more time to adjust."

"Okay, one more week. But only for you. I already know I want her to stay with us forever." Alyson hugged me, then rubbed my back with long, sweeping strokes. I knew she was trying to reassure me, and I licked her other hand.

"I know. Let's do something different today. I've got to check out a new beach location for a shoot that's coming up soon," Dave said, picking up his camera bag. "Let's introduce Kat to the beach together. I bet she's never seen sand before."

"Ooh yes, that sounds like a good idea. I've been longing to take her to Angrinha beach in the morning, but her legs still aren't quite strong enough to walk all that way and back yet. And that day she ran off from us. We never actually got onto the sand, as it was too busy."

"This is a small, quiet beach near Sagres. The couple want a lifestyle shoot there as they're staying in a hotel nearby. I need to suss out what the layout is like before the day."

"Sounds perfect, let's go!" Alyson jumped up, and I followed her. *I don't know what a beach is, but it sounds interesting.* She put my harness on and walked me out to the car. She opened the door, and I took a deep breath and leapt up onto the seat. *There, that wasn't too bad. I need to show them I can do everything they want me to do. Especially if Dave isn't sure about me yet.*

"Hurray, she jumped up into the car on her own. Her legs are getting stronger. Clever girl." Alyson ruffled the fur on my head and grinned at me. "Well done, little one," she whispered so that only I could hear her. She kissed me on top of my nose and climbed into the car.

"It's about forty minutes away. Settle down, Kat, we'll soon be there." Dave started the engine, and we were off. I tried to keep calm and not look at everything rushing past the windows. Alyson adjusted something on the dashboard and a pleasant rush of cold air blasted through the car to me. I must have dozed off, because suddenly we were there. Dave pulled into a car park and I stared out of the window. All I could see was blue sky, as Alyson hooked on my lead before letting me jump down.

I sniffed the air, and the hairs along my back prickled. It smelt different here. Fresher. Tangy. The scent of pine trees, lots of salt, and a wonderful smell of fish rippled across my nose. And other aromas I couldn't even name.

We walked over to a wooden bridge, and I found the perfect post for a wee. I snuffled everything as I trotted along. The sky was a bright blue, reflecting on a vast expanse of water, and beside it was a big patch of gold. We walked across a wooden path and down some steps. I hesitated at the bottom.

"It's sand, Kat. This is a beach. It's okay, it won't hurt you." Alyson unhooked my lead. "There you go. You can explore it all at your own pace. Come on."

I took a step forward, slowly putting my front paws down. I blinked in surprise. My feet sunk into the sand. It was soft and settled between my toes. I bent down to sniff it.

A-tish-oo! I sneezed loudly. It had all gone up my nose. I scuffed my nose with my paw and sneezed again. Alyson laughed at me. *Right, must remember not to breathe in when I sniff this stuff.*

I lifted my nose up and investigated the air. It was intoxicating. The blood rushed to my head as I stood there, taking it all in. *I'm alive, in this magical place.*

Suddenly, I leapt forward, enjoying the sensation of the sand beneath my paws. I ran, skidding round in a big circle, then plopped down to lie on the ground. I rolled over on my back, waving my paws in the air, and wriggled from side to side. It was scratchy and invigorating. *Marvellous.*

I ran off again, the breeze gently whipping across my face. I stopped and stared at the water. It was a little scary. Alyson told me they were called waves. They were tipping and whirling, curling into white cones as they reached the shoreline. They made a noise too, like a deep growl, with a boom sounding as each one rocked and crashed down into the water. I wasn't sure about them and kept away from the edge. I was happy where I was.

The sun warmed my back as I dug my paws into the sand. *I wonder what's underneath? How far down can I get?* I swept the sand behind me and it shot up in a fine spray as I powered through it. It was great fun, powder-soft and yielding, as I picked up speed with my paws, scrabbling and scooping, the hole getting deeper. The sand was cooler underneath, and firmer. I looked around, satisfied I had burrowed far enough, and sank into the hole, panting.

"You've got sand all over your nose, little one." Alyson sat beside me and put her arm round me. "You certainly look like you're enjoying yourself."

Dave chuckled. "She's dug a big enough hole. She was scraping and shovelling her paws like a lunatic."

I pricked up my ears. *Did he just say Luna?*

"Hang on, did you see that? When you said the word lunatic? Her ears shot up. And her face changed. Lunatic. Luna." Alyson was staring at me.

I tipped my head to one side.

"That word seems to mean something to her. Luna is a common name. It means moon. I wonder if that was her name before? She definitely reacted to it."

Too right I did. I felt a shiver crawl along my back. *That's not a name I want to remember.*

"Well, if it was her name, I don't think she liked it very much. She must have some terrible memories tucked away inside her, poor thing."

"At least she has a new name now. Kat the dog seems to suit her so well. Little monkey that she is." Alyson jumped up, and I leapt around her, eager to leave the name Luna far behind me.

We walked the length of the beach, and Dave took lots of photos of us. Then it was time to head back to the car. I had a last glance at the beach before we left. Inside, I was a young puppy again. It had been such fun digging and racing around.

Alyson gave me some water. I drank thirstily, then looked down

into the bowl. There was a pile of sand swirling around in the bottom.
That must have come out of my nose!

We arrived home, and I collapsed onto my bed after I had eaten my dinner. All that running and digging had worn me out. I fell asleep upside down with my legs in the air, and the last thing I heard was Alyson saying, "Look at our little girl. Fast asleep like that. She certainly enjoyed herself on the beach today, scampering around and digging that big hole. She's such a darling. I love her so much."

CHAPTER SIXTEEN

"It's your birthday soon. What do you want for a present? I never know what to get you." Dave was busy tapping away on his computer and glanced over at Alyson and me as we entered the office.

"There's only one thing I want, and you already know what that is. I want us to adopt Kat, of course." She sat on the floor beside me as I curled up on my nice, comfy bed.

"Okay then, you call Ginie and tell her the good news."

"Great. I'll do it right now, before you change your mind."

Dave rolled his eyes and carried on typing.

Alyson grabbed something, and I heard a ringing noise. I shot up and looked around. I could hear a voice. It was the lady that found me. Ginie. *Where is she? I can't see her. She must be hiding.* I walked out into the hallway. *I can't hear her now. How strange.* I ran back into the office. *Yes, she's in here. But where?*

Alyson was laughing and waved a small metal object at me. "It's my mobile phone. Ginie's here, I've got her on speakerphone," she said. *How can she be squashed into that little thing?* I shook my head. Sometimes humans confused me.

"Yes, I know. What can I say? I knew the moment I saw that photo of her you posted up on Facebook. Those eyes."

My ears pricked up. I realised this was an important call.

Ginie was talking again. Her voice was different, fainter, but I knew it was her. "Oh, I already knew you would take her. That's why I gave you all her papers and her passport when you left here." She chuckled, and my heart raced. *Is this what I think it is? Does this mean they're going to keep me?*

"Right, that's settled then. It's all official. Kat the dog is ours forever." Alyson beamed. Her smile lit up her whole face and her eyes were shining. I settled down beside her.

"Thank you so much, Ginie. We'll always be so grateful to you for stopping that day and rescuing Kat. Don't worry, we'll take such good care of her. We love her so much."

"I know you do. She's a very special girl. I knew I had to find a special family for her. Have a wonderful life with her, and I'll come and see you soon."

Alyson ended the call and reached over and gave me a hug, almost squeezing the air out of me. She smiled at me and said, "Come over to the sofa and sit with me. I want to have a little chat with you." She stood up and picked up a blanket, walked into the lounge, and put the blanket on the sofa beside her. I followed, padding along behind her. She patted the seat and said, "Come on, Kat. Jump up."

I hesitated for a second, making sure I understood her. I didn't want to get in trouble for sitting on the furniture. Then I hopped up and settled down on the blanket beside her. It was lovely, all squishy and soft. It was great to be sitting high up, too.

Alyson put her arm around me as Dave walked in and laughed.

"Oh, I see. Five minutes after we've adopted her, and she's already lying on the sofa. She'll be sleeping on your bed next."

"Well, actually…" Alyson's voice trailed off.

"No. No sleeping upstairs. She's got a perfectly good bed in the kitchen." Dave shook his head and went back into the office.

"Ha, that's what he thinks, little one. Shh, don't say anything. Little steps, eh? We'll have you sleeping on my bed at night soon, you wait and see," whispered Alyson, the mellow warmth of her body nestled beside me. I stretched my legs out.

"Right, let me tell you some things, my darling girl. You don't know how long I've wanted a dog of my own to love. When I was a little girl, we always had a dog at home. First up was Jane. She was wonderful. A Dalmatian crossed with a spaniel. All black and white, with spots everywhere. Jane was a sweetie. I can remember sitting in a playpen like a lobster pot with her, playing with my toys. She was with us for a very long time until I was about eleven."

I tried to picture everything as Alyson carried on telling me about her childhood. Her voice was soft and almost distant as she remembered her story.

"Next was Trixie. She was a very fat Labrador. A friend of the family was ill and they couldn't keep her anymore, so she came to stay with us. She was quite old, and she didn't live very long. Which is why we won't let you get too fat, young lady."

I looked up at her, not really understanding what she was saying, but enjoying the fact she was giving me all her attention and stroking me.

"Then came Susie. She was completely bonkers. Another Labrador. We had her from about twelve weeks old. A man arrived at our house with two puppies, both yellow Labradors. I begged my mom to let us keep both of them, but she just laughed and said I had to pick one. It was an impossible decision. One pup was well behaved. The other was naughty. I took that one outside in the garden and she tried to eat all the plants. Then she started chewing on Mom's slippers. Guess which puppy I chose? Yep, the naughty one. And she spent her whole life after that being mischievous. She ate everything, even chewing through the concrete wall of our lounge, trying to get outside. She destroyed plants, cushions, shoes, toys, everything. And I loved her so much."

Alyson tapped me on the head. "No getting ideas like that of your own, eh? You've been brilliant since you arrived here. You seem to know which things are yours and what's ours. I can't imagine you would ever chew anything or be naughty."

I snorted, which made Alyson laugh. *As if I'd do something like that?*

"I do believe you understand what I'm saying, don't you?" I got a big hug for that and settled in closer, snuggling my head against her leg.

"I went off to university and got married. I was far too young, really. We had a rescue dog first, a collie crossed with goodness knows what. Minstrel. He was a dear thing at first, so playful."

Alyson's face clouded over and she picked at the edge of a cushion.

"And then one day, my first husband had to go off to a swimming competition. We loaded up the boot of the car with his things, and Minstrel watched everything happening. He must have thought we were both leaving, and that triggered something in his brain. I didn't realise at the time, but I guessed later someone must have abandoned him before. Perhaps they drove away and left him behind. I'll never know." Alyson's voice wavered.

"Anyway, I stooped down to hold his collar as the car moved off, and Minstrel whipped around. He snarled and growled, then leapt up and bit me. Right on the face. Just below my eye. I was so shocked I stood up, but his mouth was still hooked into my cheek. I had to prise his jaw open to release his grip on me."

Alyson stared out of the window. She suddenly seemed far away, remembering what had happened to her. She touched her cheek with her fingertip. "And that's why I have this scar here on my face. They rushed me to hospital and stitched me up. Seventeen stitches. The cut was only two millimetres from the corner of my eye. They said I was very lucky."

Her mouth wobbled, and her eyes filled with tears. "Do you know the worst part, though? The police insisted Minstrel was put down. They said he was a danger, and he might bite someone again. We had a young family living next door to us and they couldn't risk it. I never saw him again. My injury meant I couldn't even cry properly for him. The swelling on my face and eye. It was pretty bad."

She shrugged, and I nestled in, licking her hand.

"After Minstrel, we had two Cavalier King Charles Spaniel pups. Sam and Barney. My marriage didn't last very long, and the saddest thing for me was I had to leave them behind when I moved. I was in the police, you see, and they gave me a posting in Devon. The only place I could rent was a tiny flat, and I couldn't take the boys with me. I missed them so much."

I tried to follow her story, but mostly I just heard the sorrow in her voice.

"I threw myself into my work, and that's where I met Dave. He was a police officer too. We fell in love and got married, but we worked such crazy hours. It wouldn't have been fair to have a dog, so I waited almost eighteen years. And then we moved from the UK to here in Portugal, and we had the time and space for a dog. Finally. We contacted Ginie and told her what we wanted, and she said she'd find us the perfect dog. And she did. And here you are."

She leaned over and hugged me, and I felt her body shudder. She wiped her hand over her eyes and sniffed. I huddled in even closer, wanting to show her I loved her, and licked her hand again.

"Now you're ours, and I am going to love you so much. I'm going to be your mommy, and no-one is ever going to hurt you again. And I am never ever going to leave you." She kissed the top of my head and scratched me behind my ears, her face awash with tears as she bent down to hug me.

I loved the idea of having a human mommy. It sounded wonderful, and I enjoyed being stroked and held, too. I fell asleep, snuggled into her arms, the blanket and soft sofa beneath me, and dreamed about the beach. My awful life at the farm and all those terrible memories faded away, replaced by thoughts of a future filled with walks and bowls of food and soft kisses on my nose.

CHAPTER SEVENTEEN

The next morning, they went out and left me in the kitchen, promising to be back soon. Dave closed the gate, and I sat on my bed as they left. Luckily, they didn't leave the radio on, so it was nice and quiet as I settled down. The front door clunked shut, and I wriggled around a few times, trying to get comfortable.

That sofa was soft, perfect for snoozing on. I wonder if I can open the gate? I had watched Dave several times as he slid the bolt across the top; it slipped into a little hole in the wall. I padded over to the gate, sniffing it cautiously. I balanced on two legs, putting my front paws on top of the gate, and looked at the bolt. *Shouldn't be too difficult, if I grip it with my teeth.* I reached over and grabbed it, but it was quite small and I couldn't quite hold it. I tried again, more slowly, and it slithered across. I stepped back and pawed the gate, pulling it towards me. *That was easy.*

The gate swung open, crashing into the far wall. *Oops! They'll know I've opened it now. What if I close it again?* I stepped out of the way and pulled it shut with my paw. It had a little catch that held it in place and stopped it moving, which meant I could stand up on my hind legs and slide the bolt back with my teeth. *Perfect. Now they will never know.*

I curled up on the sofa and fell asleep.

A car pulled up opposite the house. I could usually sense their approach long before I heard the car, but I must have been sleeping so soundly I missed the signs. I shot off the sofa and sat on the floor, trying to appear innocent.

Alyson walked in first, carrying a big bag, which she set down on the floor. She looked over at me and laughed.

"What are you doing out here? I thought you were on your bed in the kitchen?"

I wagged my tail and resorted to my cute look, tipping my head to one side and peering up through my lashes.

Dave came crashing through the door and almost tripped over the bag Alyson had put on the floor.

"I thought we left Kat in the kitchen? I was sure you closed the gate?" Alyson strode over to the gate. "It's locked. So how did Kat get out? She couldn't have jumped over it?"

"No, I definitely locked it. I remember doing it." Dave scratched his head. "So, how did she end up in the lounge?"

"Well, she must have opened it. And, erm, then closed it again behind her." Alyson chuckled. "She's one clever girl." She strolled into the lounge and put her hand on the sofa.

How did she know where I had been sleeping?

She smiled at me as Dave dumped the bags in the kitchen. "Mmm, who's been asleep on the sofa, then?" She patted me on the head and winked at me, and I breathed an enormous sigh of relief. I wasn't in trouble. *But how did she know?*

It was as if she could read my mind. "The seat's warm, Missy."

Whoops! Busted. But it didn't seem to matter too much. Dave came into the lounge. "We might as well get rid of the gate. If she has worked out how to open it. And shut it again. Cheeky thing."

"Yes, I don't think we need it anymore. It's not as if she's naughty when we're out. I guess she wanted to sleep on the sofa. Can't say I blame her. Let's put a rug on this seat, and she can sleep in here." Alyson patted the spot I had been sleeping on and winked at me again. "Your secret's safe with me, little one."

My legs were soon strong enough for me to climb stairs easily. I went up and down the steps to the garden, and once ventured upstairs to have a look around, but one thing still frightened me. Those stairs by the kitchen that disappeared down to the garage. Alyson took me over to them one morning.

"Come on, let's see what's there. It won't hurt you; I promise." She switched the light on, and I peered down, my nose twitching.

"They're just stairs, like the other ones. It'll be okay. I need you to get used to being in the basement. That's where I work, and I want you by my side each day."

I followed Alyson. It was the corner that bothered me; it was so dark, but once I reached the turning, I could see another set of steps and a doorway that was open. I sped down and soon reached the bottom. I peered round the door and stopped still. *Wow, it's enormous in here. And so bright.*

The room was divided into two parts. I turned left and walked into a big wide area full of equipment and boxes, with a table at the end.

"That's Dave's photo studio, Kat. But come and see the other end." Alyson called me over and I walked round, sniffing everything. There was a big glass door, and I could see out into the garden.

"This is my studio, where I paint. And this sofa can be yours. You can lie here and watch me work." She patted the seat next to her, and I jumped up and sat beside her. "That's my easel, and those are my paintings on the wall. I'll sneak you into my next exhibition, and you can be my lucky charm and help me sell them."

I didn't really know what she meant, but I could tell how happy she was, and I settled down to watch. She put some music on and set out lots of things on the table beside the easel.

Oh dear, what's that noise? It sounded like a bat screeching, and I looked up, expecting to see one circling overhead. *I'm not sure my mom is very good at singing. Oh well, I think I'll go to sleep and leave her to it.* I closed my eyes as the smell of paint filled my nostrils.

After that, we went down to Alyson's studio most mornings after breakfast. She painted, and I snoozed, waiting for eleven o'clock each day. That was coffee time, and I always got a biscuit, as Dave and Alyson sat chatting.

I liked our days; we had a nice routine for them. Get up, go for a walk with Alyson, have breakfast. Go to the studio, coffee time with a yummy biscuit for me at eleven, and another snooze. Quick walk for a wee before lunch, out again in the afternoon. Home for tea, another snooze, bedtime walk, then time to sleep. It was perfect.

One morning Dave came into the studio and said to Alyson, "I need to go to Lagos this afternoon and take some photos of the view from Ponte da Piedade for a magazine. Why don't I take Kat with me? It'll be a lovely walk for her."

"Yes, that would work. I've got to pop into town later, anyway. Just take care of her."

"Of course I will." Dave tutted.

We set off after lunch, Dave putting his camera gear in the boot of the car. I looked back and saw Alyson waving as we drove off, and I sank my head down on my paws. It was weird going out without her, but I cheered up when we arrived at a car park, and I jumped out. We were right on top of the cliffs, and I sniffed the air. It was so fresh; the wind was blowing from the south, and it was full of unusual scents and spices.

Dave grabbed his bag and a metal thing he called his tripod, and we marched along the cliff path. That tripod was a strange contraption. It looked quite small until Dave put it on the ground and pulled at it. Three long metal poles shot out sideways and he stabbed them into the soil. I backed away from it.

"It's fine. It can't hurt you. Here, let me clip your lead onto my belt, then I don't need to hold on to you. I'm going to take some shots of the cliffs."

I stood watching for a while. I had been out before when Dave had his camera with him and I knew I had to stand behind him, but I soon yawned and started sniffing around. Lots of birds had been there recently, and I followed a trail that was quite fresh. It led all the way to the edge and down the side of the cliff. I leant forward, trying to sniff further.

Suddenly, my front paws slipped. The soil was soft, full of tiny green plants that moved under my feet. My back legs lost their grip, and I pitched forward. *My head is too low.* I scrabbled with my front paws, but that only made things worse as I hurtled forward. *Help, I'm going to fall.*

My back legs skidded, and I looked down. The beach at the bottom of the cliffs seemed a very long way away. I shuddered. *Is this it? I'll never survive that drop. Help!*

I toppled further forward. The view spun in front of me, a swirling kaleidoscope of colours and shapes, as I gasped and closed my eyes.

A sharp tug jolted my neck. I winced in pain. My legs left the ground, and I was hoisted up into the air. I whirled around and yelped.

Dave had hold of me. I squirmed, wriggling my legs.

"It's okay, I've got you. You're alright."

My feet touched the ground as he dropped me back down. I panted and shook my head. I moved away from the edge and licked my grazed pads.

"Phew, that was a bit close, young lady. Good job I had you hooked onto my belt. I can't imagine what your mom would have said if I'd returned home without you." He packed up his camera gear and looked over at me. I was still slumped on the ground, trying to get my breath back. "I tell you what. It can be our secret, eh? Let's not tell your mom what happened."

Dave listened to loud rock music on the car stereo all the way home. I wondered if they made ear plugs for dogs. Then I had an idea. *They'd be perfect for when Alyson is 'singing' in her studio too!*

"Did you have a good time?" Alyson rushed over to give me a hug as soon as I walked in the door. "I missed you, darling girl. Was she alright? Did she behave herself?"

"Erm. Well yes. Apart from when she tried to dive off the cliff."
Dave dropped his camera bag onto the kitchen table.

"What?" Alyson's face contorted, her eyes wide. She folded her
arms.

Yes, what? I thought we'd agreed not to mention that? I watched with
interest as the conversation unfolded and Dave explained what had
happened.

"Well, I hope you realise if you'd come home without her, I'd have
sent you packing?"

"Yes, I wouldn't even have bothered coming back here. I'd have just
driven straight to the airport and caught the first flight out of
Portugal. I know how much you love our girl. I love her too. She gave
me quite a fright."

"That's the last time you get to take her out with you when you're
shooting."

"Yes, I thought you might say that."

I settled on my bed and closed my eyes. *That suits me, it was pretty
boring stood there, anyway.* I fell asleep and dreamt I was on the top of a
cliff, falling down and down, my legs cycling round and round in
mid-air. I woke with a jump seconds before I reached the ground.
Better not try to sniff things too close to the edge next time.

CHAPTER EIGHTEEN

That night I sat on my bed as Alyson and Dave ate their dinner in the kitchen. I had already eaten my food, but I stayed alert, in case they dropped anything. They did not let me scrounge or beg from the table, which was a shame, as I knew my soft brown eyes looking hungry were irresistible to them. I know, because Alyson told me. But she also explained their food was bad for me, so apart from the occasional titbit at lunchtime, I never got very far with them at mealtimes.

After they had cleared up, I snuggled on the sofa, sat between them on my blanket. I had just fallen asleep when a loud noise made me jump. The funny screen on the wall was shining, full of colours that moved and sparkled. And the noise it made too! There were people talking, but there was no-one in the lounge except Dave and Alyson. I looked up at them; they were both staring at the screen. Neither of them seemed worried about it. I shook my head. Sometimes humans were strange.

Bedtime came, and it was time for my last walk of the day with Alyson. The night sky was shining, the stars glittering and twirling as I sniffed the air. Everything was still and quiet, and I shivered. It was much colder now at night. My claws clacked on the pavement as we walked. Alyson made a 'whooo' sound as she rubbed her hands together and hopped from foot to foot as I stopped to sniff a tree.

"Come on, Missy, quick wee tonight, then straight home. It's too cold to stay out here for long."

We hurried back inside, and I waited for my 'bedtime Bonio', as Alyson called it. A lovely fat crunchy biscuit. I scoffed it and licked my lips, checking the floor in case I had dropped any crumbs.

Then another surprise. "Up to bed. It's too cold for you to stay down here in the kitchen, even with a blanket over you. Time for you to snuggle up with me."

Dave chuckled. "So, she's off up to bed with you, is she? I knew she'd get there in the end."

"Yes, it's too cold for her down here." Alyson's face was beaming. Her smile lit up her eyes as she looked at me. "Come on, little one."

She set off up the stairs and I followed her, my paws tripping up the steps in my haste to climb up behind her. We walked into her bedroom, and she patted the bed. There was no need to offer a second time. I jumped up straight away and perched on the end. I waited while she went into the bathroom, then changed her clothes. *How strange. She wears different things at night. I wonder why?*

Alyson climbed into bed and called me over to her. I was unsteady on my legs as my paws sunk into the mattress. It moved underneath me and I swayed. *This is weird. It looks firm, but when I stand on it and try to walk, everything moves.* I sat down, puzzled.

"It's okay, don't worry. It's a waterbed. Come and lie up here beside me. You'll feel how warm it is. Here you are. This pillow is for you."

I crawled up and put my head on the soft padded cushion. I stretched out and relaxed as Alyson covered me with a fluffy blanket. The mattress underneath me had a gentle heat coming from inside it. I couldn't believe it. I was here with my alpha, my pack leader, in this comfortable space, and all I had to do was fall asleep. I felt like I was a little puppy again, lying beside my birth mother, safe and loved. No-one could attack me here. The cold weather was outside, and this was my home now. I could stop worrying about whether this would last.

Alyson had told me so many times she loved me and that this was my 'forever home' and finally I believed her. My tummy was full of food, and as she kissed my nose and said, "Night, night, little one, sweet dreams," I let out a deep sigh, closed my eyes and fell asleep.

The next morning I woke as the first embers of daylight tiptoed across the sky and in through the window, inching their way across the bed until they reached me. Alyson yawned and tousled the top of my head as she stretched her arms out wide.

"Time for a walk," she said, climbing out of bed. I licked my paws and waited as she changed her clothes again, then I leapt off the bed and padded downstairs.

Outside the house, she stuffed my lead in her pocket as she wrapped herself up in a big coat. "I don't think you need that anymore. I've got it in case, but you walk so nicely beside me, and it's very early in the morning. There's no-one around."

We set off down the road. "I reckon your legs are strong enough now to make it to the village and back. Let's see how far you can go, eh? We might even make it to the beach today."

I stopped to sniff lots of things along the way. I loved the fact Alyson never minded when I halted; she said it was funny watching me. I wished I could explain to her how important it was that I checked everything out; it was crucial to know what had happened overnight. There were so many markers and messages to read and decipher with my nose. It often took me a long while to get to where we were heading, but Alyson always waited for me.

We reached the village, and my tail quivered. This was a whole new world to explore, with houses and shops, and patches of grass, all full of unfamiliar scents and signs. The river ran through the village; the water gurgling and bubbling as it galloped along a concrete path built into the ground. I peered over the edge and looked down, fascinated by the movement and noise the water made.

Pigeons skipped along the pavement, and I raced after one, but it soared off into the air, its wings flapping as it sounded a warning cry, "Coo—coo." Unlike the seagulls that I still tried to avoid; I liked the pigeons. I wished they would play with me, but every time I ran up to them, they flew away.

We turned a corner where the river widened, and wriggled through a narrow alleyway. I gasped as we reached the other end; we were walking on a sandy path. I recognised it as the one we had visited that day the seagull had frightened me. I looked up and saw several of them whirling overhead.

"It's okay, they won't hurt you. If we walk over here, we'll be on the beach." Alyson made her way over to a small path woven between the sand dunes.

I scampered after her and stopped at the top, looking down. Ahead of me was a stretch of pristine golden sand and, beyond it, the sea. The sky above had turned to a crisp, icy blue, and there wasn't a soul around. Just us. The only marks in the sand were the footprints made by the seagulls, and it was soft underfoot as I scampered across the beach. The spray from the waves caressed my face as I raced ahead, carried by the breeze, and I whirled around. I was free. Unfettered. My heart swelled. It was heavenly.

I spied a seagull ahead of me on the sand. He had his back to me, and I glided up to him, slowly tipping my paws forward. The hairs on the back of my neck furled up, a section at a time. I paused, my front right paw dangling in the air, and held my nose high. I could smell the bird from here. A deep, pungent, almost acrid stench of rotten fish and poo filled my nostrils, and I quivered.

"Go on, chase after him," Alyson whispered. "Show him who's boss."

I crouched, then leapt off the ground, racing towards the seagull. I almost reached him when he whirled around, his wings beating as he lifted into the air, squawking a warning call at me.

That was fun! I spotted another one further along the beach and chased after it, my tongue lolling, my mouth breaking into a wide grin. That one flew off, too. *So they are frightened of me after all.* I realised they didn't pose a threat to me as I sank down onto the sand, panting, and waited for Alyson to catch me up.

We sauntered back through the village until we reached the massive hill that led to our house. My legs were sore from all that running on the sand, and I stared up at the steep incline in dismay. *I'm not sure I can climb that.*

"Don't worry, there's a shortcut. This way." Alyson turned right and headed off along a narrow lane. *She's reading my mind again.* I trotted after her and we walked through a little estate of houses. The slope here was only gentle, and before I knew it, we had arrived at the top of the hill on the main road. I could almost see our house. I stopped for a drink of water, happy to rest my paws for a few minutes.

As soon as we got home, I devoured my breakfast, then settled down for a sleep. In my dreams, the seagulls were whirling around my head, and I was flying in the sky beside them. But when I tried to play with them, they flew away. I never worried about seagulls again after that, and looked forward to racing along the beach every morning trying to catch one.

CHAPTER NINETEEN

"I think Kat's due a haircut soon." Alyson was on the sofa beside me, her hand stroking my ears as Dave looked over and nodded.

"I know the groomer Ginie used has moved away, so we'll have to find someone else. It's a shame to cut all her beautiful curls, but the weather is getting warmer now. She won't want all that heavy weight once summer comes." Alyson looped her fingers through my fur and smiled at me.

"I did a photo shoot for a couple last week and they mentioned they had dogs. They said something about a groomer as well. I can ask them."

I didn't like the sound of that. My fur bristled. I wasn't exactly a fan of having my fur trimmed, not after the way the farmer had attacked me with a pair of old rusting metal clippers. I was so weak when Ginie found me I hardly noticed the groomer that time, but I listened carefully as Dave made some phone calls.

"All booked in for next week. They sounded nice, very professional."

I knew something was up even before I jumped in the car. We were off somewhere different, I could tell, and I wasn't sure what to make of the atmosphere in the car. It didn't help my mood when I heard Alyson say to Dave, "I hope she'll be okay. I wonder if they'll let me stay while they trim her?"

"She'll be fine. Don't worry. We can leave her with them and pop over to Faro and do some shopping, then pick her up afterwards."

"Mmm, I'd rather stay with her if I can. We'll have to see what they say."

I shrank lower in my seat as Dave parked up and Alyson opened the door and unhooked me. I peered out. A big concrete building stood to one side of the car park, and dogs were barking inside. *I don't like the feel of this.* I huddled backwards, but Alyson called to me and I jumped down, staring around and sniffing. *This is a terrible place. How can I tell them, though?*

Alyson had my lead in her hand, and I trudged behind her. We walked through a door and a strong chemical smell hit my nose. A man greeted us and we stood waiting. Another door opened, and a woman walked into the reception area and shook Alyson's hand.

The next thing I knew, I was being led away. The woman had hold of my lead and I looked back at Alyson and Dave, my eyes wide. *No. Don't leave me here with her. I don't like this place.*

"Are you sure I can't stay with her? I'm sure she'd be happier if I was with her?" I could hear the catch in Alyson's voice as she took a step towards me, almost pleading with the woman.

"She will be fine. Come back in two hours." The woman led me through the door, which slammed shut behind us, and I took a step backwards.

The room had two metal tables and a sink. On the far wall was a set of cages, with four small dogs in total inside them. Three of the dogs were whining, and the fourth had huddled down in its cage, eyes darting from side to side. *This is horrible. What are those dogs doing in there? And what's going to happen to me?*

I whined and pulled back against my lead, trying to escape.

"No, you don't. Come over here, let's get started." The woman hoisted me up onto a table and hooked a strap around my neck and another in front of my back legs, under my tummy. The surface was shiny, and my paws slipped as I tried to get a firm purchase as I stood there. A low hum came from a machine, then a deafening whining noise as the clippers whirred into life. She slid them across my neck as she clasped my head in place, her fingers pinching my skin.

My breath came in ragged gasps, and I forced myself to remain calm. At least the clippers didn't hurt me, as I squirmed my head round, trying to free myself from her tight grip.

The torture seemed to last for ages. The machine whirred as the clippers skimmed across my body and my lovely curls fell onto the table around my feet. The woman grasped each of my legs in turn, twisting them high into the air. I yelped as she grabbed the side of my leg where the farmer had beaten me, but she took no notice of me at all. Her mouth formed an angry line across her face as she glared at me. She didn't say a word to me as she held the clippers with one hand and gripped me with the other.

She moved to my tail, and I reared up, trying to stop her, but she held me so tight I couldn't move as she skimmed the machine over my bum and underneath me. I winced in pain. Her fingers were digging into my side, and every time I moved, the metal blade of the machine cut into me.

She swept my fur off the table with her hand and switched off the machine. A young girl entered the room and cleaned up as the woman grabbed me under my body and hoisted me up. She walked over to an empty cage, pushed the door open with her elbow, then shoved me inside. The door closed with a loud clang, trapping me inside. The space was so tiny I could hardly turn round. I wanted to lick my stomach and bum, which were stinging and sore.

The woman grabbed one of the other dogs and placed him on the table. Not once did she speak to the little dog, who was shaking all over, as she trimmed his fur. I closed my eyes, trying to block out everything that was happening, but the sound of the little dog whimpering interspersed with the constant squealing and whirring of the machine made it impossible for me to settle.

The young girl lifted out the dog from the cage next to me and dropped him into the big sink in the corner. There was a tap and hose attached to the wall, and she washed the dog, covering him in shampoo, then rinsed it all off. The dog shook himself as she finished and she shouted at him, then grabbed a towel and covered the dog from head to foot, rubbing briskly. The dog was struggling under the towel, trying to free his head to breathe.

This is a nightmare. I hope it's over soon. How could Alyson and Dave leave me here? I shrank down in the cage and tried to get comfortable, but it was impossible. The floor stank of urine, and I licked my paws to remove the foul odour.

Soon it was my turn to be dumped in the sink. The shampoo was awful, flowery and sickly, and the suds splashed across my face. My eyes stung, and I tried to twist my head away, but I had a strap tied to my collar and I couldn't move. The girl massaged me, then hosed off the shampoo.

She lifted me onto a mat on the floor and I took a deep breath as she loomed over me with a towel. I was bigger than the other dog, though, and the towel didn't reach my head as she rubbed my back and legs with a rough, jagged motion. She patted my face, then lifted me onto the table, hooking me up again.

"That's not dry enough," the woman snarled at the young girl. "I need another towel."

She grabbed a dry towel from a pile on the other table and threw it over my back, pummelling me as she dragged it from side to side and underneath me. I staggered, losing my footing, and skidded over, teetering on the edge of the table, my neck still caught in the strap. My claws scrabbled on the shiny surface. I gasped. *I can't breathe.*

"Oh, for goodness' sake, why can't you stand still?" The woman seized my back legs and pulled me backwards, twisting her nails into my body. I yelped in pain. "You can stop that noise right now. I'll be finished in a minute, so stop whining."

She trimmed me with a pair of scissors, then put me back in the cage. She walked out of the room; the door slamming shut behind her.

It seemed an age before she returned, lifted a dog out of its cage and walked out again.

My senses came alive. Alyson and Dave were close by. The door opened, and the woman returned. I glimpsed the reception area before the door slammed shut. *Yes, it's them. They're back. Now get me out of here.*

The young girl unfastened the cage door and hauled me out, dropping me to the ground. I scrambled for the door, waiting for it to be opened, then raced over to Alyson. She bent down and grabbed me, hugging me, and kissing me all over. I squirmed in her arms, reaching up to lick her face.

"Oh, my darling. I missed you. All your gorgeous curls are gone. But you still look beautiful to me. And they'll soon grow back." Alyson sat on the floor, stroking me. Her eyes were glistening.

"I had to take it all off. You left it far too long before getting her trimmed." The woman towered over us, her arms folded.

I shrank away from her and flinched. Alyson tipped her face to one side, her eyes narrowing. Her fingers rested on my head. I sensed she was asking me what had happened.

It was terrible. That woman was cruel to me. I never want to see this place again. I tried to tell her what I was feeling, but my head sank towards my chest. It was impossible to explain.

"Yes, well, thank you very much for that advice. How much do we owe you?" Alyson stood up and reached for her purse. She marched over to the counter and paid, slamming her card down on the desk, as Dave held me close, stroking my back.

"Come on, let's go." Alyson walked over to us and attached my lead.

"Here's our brochure. Do come again." The woman approached us, a pamphlet in her hand.

"Oh, thanks, but I think it's just too far for us to travel. But thank you anyway." Alyson brushed past her, and I shot outside, relieved it was all over. I shook myself, the air cold against my body. *All my fluffy fur has gone.* I trotted over to a wooden signpost and had a long wee, flinching as I flexed my leg up in the air.

I curled up on the seat in the car and licked myself all over. *What a terrible, sickly, smelly shampoo.* My nose wrinkled up as I lay there. My tummy and bum were so sore where the clippers had grazed my skin. I squeezed my eyes shut, trying to erase the memory of the cages. And that woman. I shuddered.

"I'm not going there again. Poor Kat. Did you see her face when she came out of the door? That woman was horrible." Alyson turned to Dave as he drove along, and he nodded.

"Something about that place felt wrong. We'll probably never know what happened, but you're right. Kat certainly seemed pleased to see us, that's for sure."

"We'll have to find someone else next time." Alyson turned round in her seat and looked at me, a question in her eyes. I stared back at her and then dropped my head onto my paws. I hoped she could tell how dejected I was. My body hurt too, where the blade on the machine had nicked me, but it was the dreadful memories inside my head I wanted her to see.

"She's definitely not happy at all. Poor girl. We'll not be going back there again, that's for sure."

I settled down. *She can read me pretty well now, that's interesting. Thank goodness I won't have to go through that nightmare again.* I licked my tummy and tried to sleep as the car rattled along the road. I just wanted to go home.

CHAPTER TWENTY

Our morning walks through the village continued. I loved going out early, when everywhere was quiet and the air crisp. The sky was often a haze of orange light, broad brushstrokes of colour painted haphazardly above us, turning to a brilliant electric blue as we walked. Everything seemed bright and new, a gentle breeze wafting enticing spicy aromas across my face, the ground full of overnight scents to explore.

As soon as we reached the beach, I took off, racing ahead, chasing the seagulls, the velvet soft sand sinking beneath me as my paws skipped across the surface.

"It's low tide today. Let's go round the rocks over there and we can walk along Praia Grande beach." Alyson caught up with me, her face one big smile as she lifted her head and took a deep breath, savouring the fresh air and warm sun on her face. *She loves it on the beach as much as I do.*

My ears pricked up. Praia Grande. Alyson had been promising to show me this beach for ages. She said I had to wait until I was strong enough to manage the longer walk. *This is it. Today's the day.*

I twitched my nose and trotted forward to the water's edge and the giant rocks that divided the two beaches. The sand here was wet and even softer. My paws sunk in as we walked around, picking our way between the boulders.

A vast expanse of beach stretched ahead of us. The sand gleamed, sparkling in the sunlight, and the waves seemed enormous, crashing and tumbling to the shore. Far ahead in the distance, rugged cliffs towered over the sand. Seagulls whirled and swooped overhead, and the whole beach was deserted. It was stunning.

"Angrinha behind us is just a river beach. Praia Grande is a proper coastline and out there, that's the ocean. We won't be able to walk here in the summer once they've put out all the sun loungers and the lifeguard station. But we're fine until then. Come on, let's explore."

I loved the way Alyson chatted to me, explaining things. She told me once she wasn't certain how much I understood, but she was going to talk to me anyway. I wished I could tell her that the best part was just hearing her voice and knowing she loved me and wanted to share her thoughts with me.

I scampered along, but kept away from the edge of the sand where the waves kept rolling in. An incessant surge of white foam twirled around my paws. Out to sea, the waves made a loud boom as they crashed and tipped over, each one tumbling forward towards the shore. The water stretched far into the distance, touching the sky and merging into a haze of shimmering blue. I realised how small I was against the elements, as I sniffed the breeze and looked around me.

We walked all the way to the end, and Alyson perched on a rock as she gave me some kibble and a drink of water. She had lots of pockets in her trousers that seemed to produce everything I needed, as if by magic, including a little dish made of something that bounced back into shape when she unrolled it. Perfect for holding the water from the bottle she carried in another pocket.

We strolled home, and I stopped to have a wee as Alyson gasped and looked at the ground. "That's not good."

I sniffed behind me. My pee smelt different.

"There's a bit of blood in there. I'll have to watch that, in case something's wrong." She patted me on the head. "Don't worry, I'm sure it's nothing."

I gobbled up my breakfast and lay on my bed.

"Well, there's certainly nothing wrong with your appetite," Alyson said as she picked up my empty food bowl. "I hardly need to wash this one up. You lick it so clean every time it's shining."

Lunchtime came, and another quick walk. Another pee. And more blood.

"Oh dear, that's not looking too good." We returned home, and Alyson spoke to Dave. "I think I'm going to call the vet and get some advice."

She went to her studio and came back. "Right, I've talked to him, and he said to monitor her and if it continues tomorrow morning to take her in and he'd have a look at her. He told me not to panic; it's most likely an infection."

"Well, where could she have got that from?" Dave stared at me as he scratched his head.

Don't look at me. I don't know where it's from.

"Something's obviously not right. I'll keep an eye on her." Alyson patted me, and we only had a short afternoon stroll, then spent a quiet evening snoozing on the sofa. I went out for my night-time walk, had a quick wee, then scampered home.

The next morning, we wandered round rabbit lane. Alyson watched me like a hawk, hovering over me as I peed. It smelt acrid, like sour vinegar. I wrinkled my nose.

"Still the same," Alyson said to Dave as she walked into the house. "I'd better call the vet's and we'll take her over there."

In the car, I sensed something was wrong. I whined and Alyson tried to reassure me as we parked up outside a concrete building with enormous glass windows. Inside smelt funny. The stale scent of other dogs and cats was all over the floor and I snuffled round, trying to work out where we were.

A door opened and out stepped a man in a white coat. I remembered him from when Ginie took me to the vet's. *But how did that man get here? This isn't the same building. Does he work here now?* It was very confusing.

"Hi Olalya, how are you?" He walked over to me and patted my head. I relaxed a little, but I was still unsure of what was happening.

"Hello. She's called Kat now. And we're a bit worried about her." Alyson clenched my lead and wiped her palm down her trouser leg.

"Bring her in, and I'll take a look."

We followed him into a room with a metal table in the centre and a desk in the corner. Dave picked me up and put me on the table, and everyone crowded around me. Alyson stroked my head as the man checked me over.

"Well, she's certainly gained some weight, and she looks great."

"Ginie told me you looked after Kat really well." Dave chatted to the man. *He doesn't seem too worried.* I twisted round as the man touched my stomach and rear end. *Ouch, that hurt!*

"Yes, Ginie brought her to me after she found her, and I checked her all over. We performed her operation a week later to sterilise her." He rolled me onto my back. "It's healed nicely, too."

"So what's wrong with her? Why is she peeing blood?" Alyson's eyes were wide as she talked to the vet and her hand trembled as she fondled my ears.

"I don't think it's anything too serious. She seems in good health. It's probably just an infection."

"Where could that have come from?"

"Well, anywhere really, but usually you can trace it back to something." He stroked my tummy and his fingers stopped over the grazes that were still healing.

"She's obviously been to a groomer recently. They didn't do a very good job. Look at these marks here."

"Yes, the end of last week. We tried someone recommended to us. We won't be going there again."

"I would hesitate a guess and say that's where she got her infection from. A dirty floor, or tools not cleaned and disinfected properly. It's probably that." The vet smiled at me. "Never mind, I'll prescribe a course of antibiotics, and she'll be fine in a few days."

He strolled over to his desk and typed on his computer. He wrote something on a piece of paper and handed it to Dave. "There, that should do the trick. If it's still a problem after she's had the course of tablets, bring her back. But I'm sure it will clear up. She's a beautiful dog. You're very lucky to have her."

"I know," Alyson replied, as she scooped me up in her arms and hugged me. "We love her so much. She's a really special girl. Thank you for being nice and gentle with her."

"I'm happy to help. They're looking for a new vet, so I'm filling in. I'm only here two days a week. The rest of the time, I'm back east at my clinic. But you're welcome to come over there if I'm not here. I always like to see old patients, especially rescue ones, and to see how well they're doing in their new homes. Ginie and all the other charities do amazing work out here. I like to support them if I can."

"Yes, they sure do. We can't thank her enough for finding our girl. We'll always be grateful to Ginie for stopping that day in Spain and rescuing Kat." Alyson picked up my lead and walked to the door and I clambered after her, glad to be leaving the room. *I don't care how nice and kind he is. He's still a vet, and I want to get out of here.* I stood panting at the door.

"I think Missy wants to leave now," Alyson said, and laughed. She shook the vet's hand, and we all trooped outside.

"Bye then, and don't worry about her. Give it a week and she'll be back to normal." The vet waved as we drove away, and I settled down for the long ride home.

The next few days were fun as Alyson and Dave tried to get me to swallow the tablets the vet had prescribed. I knew when they had put the medicine in my food bowl, even though they tucked it under the meat. I carefully ate all my food around the offending item, leaving the tablet lying in the bowl. It reminded me of plastic bags and I wouldn't eat it.

"Well, that's not going to work, is it?" Dave said, shaking his head. "Let's try hiding it in a piece of ham." He opened a packet from the fridge. A heady, meaty aroma swirled across the room, and I sat drooling drops of saliva on the floor.

Dave turned his back to me. *I know what you are doing, pal. You're wrapping a slice of ham around that tablet thing.* I love humans. They think if I can't see them, I won't realise what they are doing. *Now, do I eat the ham dangling in front of my nose, or not?* It smelt heavenly. *I love ham. It's so juicy and tasty.*

The ham won. I scoffed it down, swallowing the tablet with a gulp and a shudder. But another strip of ham soon followed it, this time with no tablet tucked inside. *Okay, that wasn't too bad.* I licked my lips and looked up hopefully.

"Ha, ha, no more ham, Missy. Not now. But you can have some more later."

I was almost sorry when the tablet packet was empty. But my infection cleared up and there was no more blood, so everyone was happy, and life returned to normal. Except now they knew how much I loved ham, and sometimes Dave would open the fridge and sneak me a tender sliver.

"I saw that," Alyson said after he had just given me a particularly nice big strip of ham one day. She wagged a finger at him.

"What? I don't know what you mean!" Dave pushed the fridge door shut and winked at me.

CHAPTER TWENTY-ONE

Curling up at night on the bed next to Alyson was one of my favourite things. It was warm and safe there, with my head on my very own pillow beside her. I often stretched out one of my back legs and rested my paw against her back, barely touching her, just to reassure myself she was still there as I fell asleep.

One night, I dreamt I was chasing seagulls on the beach. I would almost reach them before they lifted up on wings that seemed as wide as the ocean, whirling away in the breeze. I raced and raced, hurtling across the sand, trying to catch them. The sun was high in the sky. It was hot and I panted, gasping for breath. I nearly tasted one seagull. My mouth was so close to its wings I could smell the remains of rotten fish caught in its feathers. At the last second, it spun round, and I snapped at the air.

I heard Alyson's muffled voice, edging its way into the corner of my dream. I stirred and rolled over in my sleep as she reached over and placed a blanket over me.

"You are a funny girl, aren't you? You must have been dreaming about rabbits or seagulls. Your little legs were whizzing around as you slept." She kissed my head as I snorted and went back to sleep.

Suddenly, my dream turned dark. The sky was black overhead,

storm clouds raced across the moon, and a chill seeped through my bones. I curled up tighter, wrapping my head around my body, but the darkness remained. I could hear gunshots and footsteps as a figure loomed over me. It was the farmer, and he was dangling a dead puppy in his hand, blood dripping from its head. I howled and tried to hide, but he kept walking towards me, the slow steady plod, plod of his boots echoing on the concrete path.

Then I was back inside the shed, water dripping from the roof onto my head, dirty sodden clumps of hay stuck to my fur. My pups were all around me. I nudged them and they rolled backwards, heads lolling, tongues hanging out. All dead. Cold as ice. I tried to warm them, bring them back to life, licking them frantically, and pawing at them. I whimpered, feeling the pain so deep inside me I thought it would rip me in half.

"There, there, it's alright, little one." Alyson's voice woke me with a start, and I jumped up, scrabbling with my paws, wondering where I was for a moment. Her arms wrapped around me, holding me in a warm, gentle embrace.

"You must have had a bad dream, darling. You were yelping and growling. It's okay now. I'm here, baby. It was just a dream; it's not real."

Her voice was soothing, and I sank back onto the mattress, still shivering and panting. I was too frightened to close my eyes in case the dream returned, as I lay there, her hand stroking my body. I tried to relax, the warmth of the bed beneath me, and the gentle caress of Alyson's voice reassuring me, as I eventually drifted back to sleep.

The next morning we walked to the beach, and Alyson squealed in delight and clapped her hands. "I've been waiting for this moment. It's low tide, and we have timed it to perfection. Come on, we can walk all the way to the end of Praia Grande beach and go around the rocks. I've always wanted to explore further along the shoreline, but the tide has never been right."

She sped off, and I raced after her, shaking my head to remove the last traces of the awful dreams of the previous night from my mind. The sky was a brilliant shade of blue, the early sunlight sparkling across the water, as we rounded the corner at the far end of the beach. I splashed through the edge of the tide, over the gleaming black rocks that lined the shore. Wisps of froth whirled around the tiny rock pools that had formed, and the air was fishy and inviting.

I padded along, then stopped dead. In front of me was an enormous cave stretching deep into the cliffs. The rocks were huge and menacing, leaning forward as if ready to touch me, and I recoiled backwards, uncertain of what to do. Then I saw them, huddled inside, perched on the ledges of rock that jutted out. Pigeons. Hundreds of them. The noise they made was deafening and the smell almost overpowering. My nose twitched as my tail stood to attention, quivering in anticipation. I was so excited I didn't know what to do.

"You can go after them, but take care. Don't go in too far."

Alyson's warning was lost on me as I ran full pelt into the cave, barking in excitement. My senses were about to explode. The sound of wings beating filled the air as the pigeons rose almost as one and flapped around the cave, cawing a warning that was almost primaeval. I was in heaven, barking and leaping up as the pigeons raced out of the entrance.

I climbed up the steep side of the cave, finding small pieces of rock to clamber along. There was a lot of slime and bird poo and my paws kept slipping. I got about halfway up and glanced back at the entrance. Alyson was waving her arms at me, whistling and calling my name.

Uh-oh. Better get down. I shuffled backwards, sliding over the last few rocks, and jumped to the ground, landing on my feet. *That was easy. Now, where are all those pigeons?*

I sniffed and checked each corner until I was certain every single bird had fled the cave, then I trotted out, satisfied with my morning's work. I clambered over the rocks, exploring further along the shore, Alyson behind me. We climbed through an archway and came across the most perfect tiny stretch of sand, surrounded by rocks, the sea tiptoeing onto the shore. Our own private beach.

We stopped, and I ate some kibble and drank a full bowl of water. I was thirsty after racing around the cave. Alyson sat on a rock, gazing out to sea, her face a perfect vision of contentment and happiness.

The sun was rising higher in the sky and it was much warmer as we set off home. I checked the cave again, making sure the pigeons hadn't returned. One solitary bird swooped out above my head, screeching in annoyance at being disturbed.

I trotted through the village, proud of the fact I didn't even need my lead anymore. I knew how far I could walk in front of Alyson, and she had taught me that if she said the word 'Close', I had to slot in and walk beside her.

We stopped at a café in the square, and I sat waiting as Alyson ate a croissant and drank a coffee. I knew she would give me more food and some water, and I gulped it down greedily. I enjoyed watching everyone walking by, as I often ended up getting some fuss or a pat on the head from many of the locals. They called me *'ovelha'* and I didn't know what that meant, but Alyson explained the word translated as 'little sheep' and that it was a nice name.

I peered at my curly black fur. *Do I really look like a sheep?* There were sheep grazing in the field near our house, but they looked nothing like me. I shook my head. Sometimes humans were hilarious.

Later that afternoon, Alyson was busy putting her washing away. The entire process always bemused me. She would take clothes out of a basket, put them in a machine, hang them outside, then bring them back inside again. I couldn't see anything wrong with the clothes, and thought they smelt better before they had been through the machine. I was drifting off to sleep, my eyes only half open.

Alyson reached into the basket and pulled out a small fluffy toy. I glanced up, but wasn't very interested. I had seen several of those things lying around the house; she had even tucked some of them in my bed in the kitchen. I assumed they were not mine to touch and avoided them.

Alyson lay on the bed, holding the toy. It was brown with orange stripes and a squashed nose, but the body was flat, and it smelt funny. Suddenly, she pressed it and a loud squeak filled the room. I shot up and looked around me. *Where did that noise come from?*

I waited for Alyson to tell me what to do. She waved the fluffy thing at me, and I heard the squeak again, this time quieter.

"It's a toy. A tiger. It makes a noise. Watch." She held it in front of me and squeezed it again. Squeak. Squeak. "It's for you. You can play with it."

She placed it on the bed, and I stretched my nose forward and sniffed. I put my paw on it and pushed it to one side. I picked it up and bit down on it. Squeak. I dropped it, startled, then grabbed it and gnawed harder. Squeak. Squeak.

This is fun. I can make the noise by myself. I nestled it between my paws and chewed on an ear. Alyson praised me. "Good girl. That's the way."

So it's alright to do this? How strange. Alyson handed me another toy. A duck. *Another one for me?* I sniffed it and grabbed it in my mouth. Squeal. It made a different noise.

"These are for you. They're your toys. You can play with them whenever you want." Alyson lay beside me, her fingers tangling in the curls behind my ear as she stroked me.

I settled down with both new toys tucked under my paws. I rested my head on the duck and fell asleep. In my dreams, I was beside my pups again, and I stirred restlessly. The barn walls closed in on me as I struggled to breathe. Then the light changed in my dream and the room filled with a soft yellow glow. My pups transformed beneath me into a stuffed duck and a little flat fluffy tiger, and I wrapped my paws around my new toys as I slept.

CHAPTER TWENTY-TWO

After that, new toys often appeared in the house. Alyson showed me each one and then left me to play with them. Soon I had a box in the kitchen where they were all stored, and I could go over and select one from the pile. But my favourites were still my tiger and the duck.

Alyson gave each of my toys a name and my job was to learn their names and fetch the correct toy if she asked for it. I enjoyed this game, although I couldn't understand why she kept pretending to lose my toys, so I had to find them for her. "Where's tiger?" always seemed a daft question to me, as I wandered over to where she had just hidden it. *He's over here, where you left him.* If the game got too boring, I just fell asleep still holding the toy in my paws. That usually did the trick.

Some days, I would take a toy with me on our walks. It all started one morning when I picked up my furry rabbit and carried it to the front door, ready for our morning walk. Alyson told me to drop it, saying I didn't need to take anything with me, but I picked it up again. Eventually she gave in, and I trotted outside, carrying the toy in my mouth, my head held high. I walked all the way to the village, holding it carefully and only dropped it for an interesting smell that needed my close attention. Alyson laughed and popped the toy in her pocket.

After that, she told me she didn't mind if I brought my tiger or rabbit along with me, as they were small and fitted in her pocket. Apparently, she drew the line at the enormous fluffy pink elephant she had bought me!

Most days, we hardly saw anyone at all on our walk, but one morning I turned the corner and stopped in amazement. It was early, and the village was swarming with people. They were covering the streets with blankets and rugs and setting up trestle tables. We carried on to the beach and by the time we returned, there were items piled all over the blankets and tables.

Alyson said it was the monthly flea market, but she pulled a funny face and winked at me. "I call it the tat market. It's full of junk and old things that no-one wants anymore. Better put you on your lead today, as it's busy."

I wrinkled my nose as we strolled past one table. It stank of dust and mildew, old musty paper, and diesel oil. *Urgh!* I sped up past that one and then paused in the middle of the street, my nose twitching. I wagged my tail. Ahead of me, on top of a blanket on the ground, was an enormous pile of cuddly toys. Just sitting there. Obviously waiting for me to play with them all.

"Oh, no you don't, Missy. I'm not taking that lot home with me," Alyson said as I pulled on my lead, trying to reach the toys. A young woman nearby laughed and came over to pat me on the head.

"Sorry, she loves cuddly toys." Alyson tried to apologise to her as I twisted my head in my collar, straining to have a closer look at everything.

"Here, let her have this one. It's an old toy my kids used to play with." The woman held out a fluffy teddy bear, and I looked up at Alyson to see if it was alright to take it.

"Are you sure? That's very kind of you. But let me pay you for it." Alyson nodded at me and I picked up the teddy. It smelt of sweets and chocolate.

"No, that's okay. She's such a darling little dog. It's on me."

I wagged my tail again as Alyson thanked her, and we set off home. I heard people saying "Oh, look at that," and "Ah, isn't she cute," as we passed by. *They're talking about me.* I held my head a little higher and trotted along, holding the teddy aloft. We reached the crossing point on the road, the place with special stripes on the ground, and I sat down. Alyson had taught me to always stop on the pavement there, as she explained the cars never stopped for us and it was dangerous.

Today, though, the cars came from both directions and halted right by the lines for us. Alyson let out a big laugh as we crossed the road. "It must be the sight of you carrying your new toy that made them stop today."

We arrived home, and I added the teddy to my storage box.

Later that afternoon, I discovered something even better than toys, cheese, or ham. We went back down to the square to a little café and Alyson bought two pots full of a white, fluffy substance. She handed one to Dave, then swiped her finger into the soft topping and reached down to me, her finger held out in front of my nose.

"Ice cream, Missy. Want to try some?"

Oh, my. I'm not sure anything had ever tasted so delicious. My tongue tingled and my mouth exploded with flavour as the creamy, cold velvet slipped down my throat. I licked my lips and smiled, looking up, hoping for some more.

"Mmm, I thought you might like that. Hang on a minute, I'll get a spoon."

She fetched a tiny plastic spoon from the counter. I soon got the hang of licking every last dollop from the spoon.

"You can't have too much, young lady. Only a tiny bit. But it can be our treat at the weekend in the summer."

It was a scorching afternoon, and the cold ice cream was soothing. It was also sweet and sticky, like nothing I had ever eaten before. I settled down after it had all gone and licked my lips. *I like living here in this village. And I love ice cream.*

We rarely saw other dogs on our morning walks, which never bothered me. I wasn't really sure how to play with them and kept my distance. I knew how to greet them, but that was about it.

Sometimes we saw a nice Irish lady, Marie, and her husband, Steve. They had two dogs. One girl was quite old and her legs jutted out at odd angles. She limped along and I never minded saying hello to her, as she was so gentle. The other dog was younger and very skittish. She flinched at the slightest noise. They were both rescue dogs, and Marie told Alyson that a rescue charity had found the younger dog locked in a shed. The poor thing had tried to escape by chewing her way through the concrete floor and had damaged all her teeth.

The other lady we often saw at the beach had a big estate car. She parked almost on the sand each morning. The first time I met her, I had a real shock as she opened the boot and dogs kept jumping out of the car. I lost count of how many there were; it was just a massive pile of fur and tails wagging and barking.

Alyson was soon chatting to her. She found out the lady's name was Dagmar and she rescued stray dogs. She had six dogs, and she brought them to the beach in batches of two or three at a time to give them a run around. Some of them were more friendly than others, and I learnt which ones I could say hello to, and which were best avoided.

Mostly, I enjoyed walking on my own with Alyson along the beach. We would see other dogs in the distance, but I liked it better when they stayed away from us. I certainly wasn't going to share my toys or ice cream with another dog!

One afternoon, there was a large Alsatian dog at the far end of the beach, barking and racing around in big circles. I hung back, sensing that it was a male dog, and he didn't look too friendly. Its owner was throwing sticks for him to fetch, then he whistled to him and they left the beach. I breathed a sigh of relief.

Alyson walked back towards the car park, and I stopped to sniff a pile of paper. Suddenly, a pickup truck carved its way along the dusty track, wheels spinning as it took off. The same Alsatian dog was sitting loose in the open cargo bed of the truck as it drove past us. He started barking at me, then leapt off the back, landing on the ground with a thump. He shook himself, then raced towards us. I growled, but I felt my heart bumping and my stomach did a somersault. He was huge and coming straight for me.

Alyson screamed, then shouted out, and I could hear the fear in her voice. I stood my ground, wedging my paws into the sand, but my whole body trembled. It seemed like an age before the dog descended on me. It was as if he was moving in slow motion, his huge paws striking the ground as the muscles on his legs rippled with each stride. As he got closer, he snarled, his lips stretched taut across his teeth. His eyes were bulging, and saliva flew out from the side of his mouth.

I braced myself as the first bite descended. His hot breath burned above my head as he growled. At the last second, I twisted away, and he missed me, his teeth crashing together as he bit into the air.

"Get away from her, you bastard." Alyson screamed and tried to kick out at the dog. I spun around, waiting for the second bite, as the dog roared at me.

"Oy, get back here!" Alyson yelled at the truck, which was driving away. The driver obviously hadn't seen what had happened.

The dog spun round and wheeled into me, pushing me sideways, and snapped at my back. His teeth grazed my fur, but he didn't get a decent grip on me as I barked at him. The speed of his attack frightened me, and I knew if he got another chance, he would bite me.

There were two people walking ahead of us and Alyson called out to them for help. One of them ran towards us and the other shouted at the driver of the pickup, which came grinding to a halt in a flurry of flying sand and squealing brakes. The driver stuck his head out of the window and glanced back. He whistled to the dog, who was standing panting and snarling in front of me.

The dog bared his teeth and took a step forward.

"Go on, get out of here." Alyson flung my lead at his head, and he turned and raced off, leaping up into the back of the truck, which disappeared in a cloud of dust.

Alyson sank to the ground beside me and enveloped me in a hug. She had tears in her eyes as she stroked me all over.

"My poor baby, are you hurt anywhere?"

I tried to reassure her by licking her hand, but I was shaking so much I slumped onto the sand, panting and quivering.

The two people came over and asked if we were alright. The man said he had taken a photograph of the truck. Alyson thanked him for their help and made a note of the registration number of the vehicle, typing it into her phone. She checked me all over, but seemed satisfied he hadn't hurt me, as she kissed the top of my head and hugged me.

"Let's go home, shall we? You were so brave, standing up to him like that and protecting me. Thank goodness he didn't bite you. It could have been so much worse." Her hand trembled as she gathered up my lead and stuffed it into her pocket.

I stood up and shook myself, and we walked home. But from that day on, I kept a wary eye out for pickup trucks and Alsatians.

CHAPTER TWENTY-THREE

The days grew warmer. Summer was just around the corner, and we strolled to the beach each day in the early morning sunshine.

Alyson had tried everything to get me to swim in the sea, but I was happier at the water's edge, where the waves gently tipped over themselves and died. Out there in the deeper water, the waves were more boisterous, crashing over the surface like boulders. I didn't like the look of that and preferred to walk along the firm sandy part of the beach, keeping a careful eye on things. Sometimes a bigger wave came thundering in, spilling white foam across the sand, and I had to make a run for it.

Alyson tossed a stick into the sea, encouraging me to fetch it. I thought that was a daft idea and proved it to her by waiting until a wave washed it back to shore. I picked it up, shook the water off it, and trotted over to her, dropping it at her feet.

"Okay, clever clogs, you win that one," she said, laughing. She threw the stick across the sand. I ran after it, picking it up again. *Hang on a minute. If I take it back to her, she'll only throw it again and I'll have to get it. I could be doing this all morning.* I ran back and sat at her feet, crunched the stick into small pieces, and looked up, waiting to see her reaction.

"Okay, I get the message. Don't bother throwing sticks." She laughed again, and I raced off ahead and dug a hole in the sand.

She took off her trainers and socks and rolled up her trouser legs. *What's she doing now?*

"Let's see if I can entice you into the water with some food." She pulled out the little bag of dog kibble she always kept in her pocket, took a handful of food, and walked over to the shoreline.

I followed her, wondering what she was doing. She strode into the water and turned to face me.

"Here Kat. Come and get some treats."

I waded out, making sure I could still feel the sand between my toes. It was cold, and I liked the sensation of the water rippling across my body, but I kept a wary eye out for the waves. I stuck my head forward to reach her outstretched hand and gobbled down the food. *That wasn't too bad.*

Alyson moved further away from me, holding out another handful of food. I could smell it, my favourite kibble. But the water was getting deeper. I placed one more paw forward, and it lifted off the ground. *Uh-oh. I don't like this.* My body was floating, and I scrabbled my paws, trying to feel the bottom again. *I don't want my kibble that much.* I wheeled around, straining back towards the shore. The firm ground reappeared beneath my feet and I sighed with relief. I shot onto the sand, shaking myself, and stared at Alyson. She waded back to shore and gave me the food, anyway.

"Never mind, little one. You did fine. Maybe next time you'll go a little deeper."

Or maybe not. She patted me on the head and sank onto the sand, stretching her wet feet and legs out in front of her.

We sat for a while waiting for Alyson's legs to dry. They glistened in the sunshine, covered in a fine layer of soft sand, as she wriggled her toes and stared out across the water. Two dogs came racing onto the beach with their owner. They were at the far end, and as they came closer, I checked them out. They seemed fine and didn't pose a threat to us.

Alyson stood up as they neared us. A lady was with the dogs, and she had a toy she kept throwing out to sea. It surprised me the toy didn't sink but floated on the surface. Both dogs bounded into the waves, swimming out and racing each other to reach the toy. The younger of the two always won and swam back with the toy in her mouth, dropping it at the lady's feet, and sat waiting for the next throw.

They were bigger than me, and apart from a cursory nose sniff from each of them, they left me alone. They both had almost straight black fur, which was wavy on the ends and long tails. I thought they might be mother and daughter, but I wasn't sure.

"Yours are Portuguese water dogs, aren't they?" Alyson patted the older dog's head.

"Yes, they are. And they love the water," the lady replied, throwing the toy for them again. The dogs bounded off, swimming out to collect it. It seemed effortless to them, and I'm sure they would have fetched it all day.

"And your little girl? She's lovely. Is she a poodle?"

Why do people always think I'm a poodle?

Alyson rolled her eyes, then smiled. "No, she's a water dog too, like yours. But she's a Spanish water dog."

The lady looked down at me, and her eyes widened. "Really? Well, I never. I didn't know there was a Spanish version. But doesn't she like the water?"

"Not really. I've no idea if she can swim or not. She prefers to walk along the beach."

"And what happened to her tail?"

"We don't know. Some Spanish water dogs are born with a short tail. Others have them docked when they're very young."

The dogs came bounding back over and shook themselves, shooting droplets of water everywhere.

I looked over at the dog nearest me. Her long tail was swishing from side to side. I didn't mind my little stump of a tail. I could wag it and it stood to attention to warn me of danger. But I envied her being able to whisk her feathery tail in the air. *It must help keep her cool, and it would be great for whooshing flies away.*

We said goodbye to them and walked home, as I pondered what I had heard. *So I'm a water dog with a tiny tail and Portuguese cousins. Well, I still don't enjoy swimming in the sea. Water dog or not.*

🐾 🐾 🐾 🐾 🐾

Dave was eating a piece of toast as we arrived home. "I've got a free day today," he said, as he cleared his plate. "Why don't we go to Alte and have a wander around? We haven't taken Kat there yet, and I'm sure she'd love it with all the ducks and the river."

"Ooh yes, that's a good idea. Give me ten minutes to get ready, and we'll go. We can have lunch there. I'll pack some things for Kat."

I pricked my ears up at that. I knew if Alyson grabbed a bowl and some food in a bag and a big bottle of water; we were in for a nice day out. Sure enough, we were soon on our way in the car, and I settled down. My senses were no longer worked up to a frenzy every time we drove anywhere, and I could relax and look out of the window.

We seemed to drive for a long time until finally we pulled up and parked on the road in front of a café. I found a nice tree and relieved myself, then trotted on the lead beside Alyson over to a table. Coffee and cake for them, and biscuits for me. Well, it was almost eleven o'clock!

After that, we wandered through the village. There were a few shops and houses, but it was very quiet. *I wonder why we've come here today?*

The road narrowed and changed to uneven cobbles. I sniffed the air. Water and a deep, earthy, fruity aroma wafted over to me. And something else. I lifted my nose higher and inhaled deeply. *Ducks.* I pulled on the lead, desperate to reach the source of the scintillating smells. We rounded a corner and a little path led down to a river. A small bridge looped over to the other side.

My nose was twitching with excitement. *Quick, come on. This way.*

The river was full of ducks, paddling and whirling around, quacking and snapping at the water with their beaks. *Yes! Let me get closer to them.*

Alyson must have read my mind as she unhooked my lead. I was free and set off straight down the slope into the water.

"Oh my gosh, we don't know if she can swim..." Alyson called out to Dave, and I heard the panic in her voice. I ploughed on and launched myself into the river. The ducks were so close I could almost sniff their bums. The water went over my head, and I panicked for a second, then my legs took over and I automatically started cycling them round in the water. I bobbed back up and shook my head to clear my eyes. *Now, where are those ducks?*

My crashing into the water had obviously scared them away. They were splashing round on the far side of the river and I swam over, desperately trying to get closer. I didn't want to hurt them. They just smelt so wonderful, and I wanted to play with them.

After a few minutes, I realised it was useless. Every time I got near to them, they swam away, effortlessly gliding across the water and bickering at me. I spotted Alyson and Dave by the slope watching me. *I suppose I'd better go back.*

A group of people came around the corner and walked to the edge of the river. As I paddled back, I could see they were all together, and most of them had cameras hanging around their necks. *I wonder if they know Dave?*

"Oh no," Alyson said. "Looks like we're about to be invaded by a tour bus company." She moved away to sit on a bench by the riverside, and Dave followed her.

There must have been about fifteen people in total crowded around as I padded up to the top of the slope. As soon as they saw me, a collective gasp went up, and they all reached for their cameras and started clicking away.

"Ah, look a doggie."

"Oh, so cute."

"I need to take a picture."

They must be talking about me. I trotted up closer to them, then stopped.

It was as if Alyson knew what I was about to do, as she cried out, "Oh no, Kat, don't do it. Not there."

Too late. My drenched coat was full of water and heavy. *Only one thing to do.* I shook myself, a good long full-body shake, all the way down to my little tail.

There was a lot of shrieking and screaming. I shook myself again for good measure, water droplets flying in all directions, then looked up. The entire party of people were shaking themselves and their cameras and crying out. *What have I done? What's the matter? Why are they copying me and shaking themselves?*

I trotted over to the bench. Alyson was laughing, holding onto Dave's arm and wiping the tears off her face. Dave's loud guffaws echoed across the riverbank. The group of people were retreating, some of them still shaking their arms and clothes as they walked away.

"Good girl," said Dave, patting me. He grimaced. "Urgh! You are wet, aren't you?" He wiped his hand on his trousers. "But well done for getting rid of all those tourists. Spoiling our nice quiet river spot."

I got a big handful of biscuits from both of them. I wasn't really sure what I had done to deserve it, but I gobbled them up, anyway.

"And now we know Kat can swim," Alyson said as she hooked my lead back on and we walked over the bridge.

Well, I could have told you that. I'm a water dog, with webbed feet, remember? I just prefer a nice calm river to swim in. Preferably one with lots of ducks for me to play with.

We walked back to the café and Alyson and Dave ordered lunch. I wolfed down the food they gave me. Swimming was hungry work.

"I'll never forget the faces of those tourists when Kat shook herself. Priceless." Dave chuckled as the waiter delivered their food.

"I know. Her coat sure holds a lot of water. I doubt they'll forget their trip today in a hurry." Alyson gave me an extra biscuit as I settled down beside her. It had been a great day out.

CHAPTER TWENTY-FOUR

Summer meant that Alyson and I got up even earlier for our morning walks. We were usually out of the door by sunrise and I loved seeing the sun peek over the horizon as we stepped outside.

My legs were stronger, and I had gained lots of weight (apparently maybe a bit too much weight!), which meant our walks sometimes lasted almost two hours. Instead of going straight down the hill to the village, we walked around 'rabbit lane' and out onto the main road. That led to a nice straight stretch of pavement, and we wriggled up through the streets to the top of town. Sometimes we walked the entire length of Praia Grande beach as well before wending our way home.

The road into town was always quiet, and apart from an old farmhouse, there were just open fields and lanes on either side of the road. I trotted along in front of Alyson one morning, off my lead as usual as there was no-one around. I was happily snuffling my way along the pavement when I suddenly stopped and sniffed ahead. *Ham. I can smell ham.*

I scurried forward, and there it was. A giant piece of ham lying on the ground. I gulped it down, then looked ahead. *There's another piece.*

And another. I couldn't believe my luck as I scampered forward, slurping up each tender slice of deliciousness.

"What are you eating?"

Uh-oh, caught in the act! I turned around, trying to hide the fact I'd been munching anything. Alyson didn't like me eating things off the floor when we were out. I didn't really understand why. I'd spent so long living rough on the streets and scavenging whatever food I could find, I considered myself quite the expert in street food. And now I was being told off for my talents. It was most bizarre.

I tried to look nonchalant, but failed miserably.

"You've eaten something, haven't you? Let me see." Alyson grabbed hold of my mouth and gently prised my jaw open. She plunged her finger inside my cheek and wriggled it around.

Oh, it was ham. That's long gone. You won't find anything in there.

"Ratty, what have you eaten? You are naughty. What if it was poisoned?"

I didn't know what that meant. It was ham, fresh ham, and it tasted fine. In fact, better than fine. It was awesome. I licked my lips. *I wonder if there's any more?*

I checked the pavement all the way to the beach, but there was no more ham. Alyson kept a close eye on me. I found an old, discarded piece of bread, but I thought better of trying to scoff that. I was in enough trouble already.

The next morning we walked the same route, but when we reached the corner of the road leading into the village, Alyson slipped my lead on and I had to trot along beside her. It was agony. I could smell the fresh pieces of ham. I pulled forward.

"What's that on the ground? Is that ham?" Alyson steered me past it with a firm, "No," as she shortened the lead. *Oh dear. No ham today then.*

I trudged slowly forward. My nose twitched, and I took a long deep breath as Alyson dragged me past each shiny slice of meat lying glistening on the ground. I started dribbling as I imagined how nice it would taste as it slipped down my throat. There was no chance of that. Alyson had her determined face on, eyes narrowed, mouth set in a line, as she hurried me past not one or two, but six pieces of ham. I counted each one.

"Why on earth are there slices of ham scattered on the pavement?"

I didn't care why they were there, I just wanted to eat them. I strained my head round in my collar, trying to reach the last piece as we walked by.

"No, sweetheart. You're not eating it. I don't know what it's doing there, and I'm not risking it in case it's bad for you." Alyson tugged on my lead.

How can ham be bad for me? I shook my head, took a last longing look backwards, and carried on to the beach.

The next morning, I was eager to get going on our walk. *Perhaps the ham will be there again, and Alyson will have forgotten about it.* No such luck. The lead went on as we rounded the corner. Ahead of us was an old man, bent over and reaching down to pick something up off the ground. He was wearing tatty old clothes and a pair of green wellies.

As we got closer to him, I realised what he was doing. He wasn't picking things up; he was dropping something. He slit open a plastic packet with a small knife, reached inside, and pulled out a slice of ham.

My mouth watered. I could smell it, juicy and fresh, full of meaty goodness. *Please let me eat it.*

"Well, that explains where the ham is coming from," Alyson said as she held back and watched what was happening. "The question is, why is he doing that?"

The answer came swiftly. A small ginger cat leapt over a low wall and sauntered along the road behind the man, delicately eating each morsel of meat.

I pulled forward, desperate to get to the ham. *All that. Just for a cat. What a waste!*

Alyson waited until the cat had finished eating before letting me walk on. I imagined each salty slice slipping down my throat as the cat leapt onto the wall and sat licking its paws. *Blasted cat. Eating it all like that*. I scoured the pavement as we walked along, in case it had missed any. *Nothing. Not a scrap left.*

"Well, at least I know it isn't poisoned meat," Alyson said as we sauntered up the hill. She stopped to speak to the man, and I stared up at the packet still dangling from his hand. It was empty. The man smelt musty and mouldy, the stench of cigarette smoke swirled around him, and I recoiled. He reminded me of the homeless man, and a shiver rippled along my spine.

That evening, Alyson grabbed her purse and my lead. "Come on, I'll make up for the ham you couldn't eat this morning. How about an ice cream?"

Dave was working and had taken the car, so we set off on foot down the hill. The village was much busier now summer had arrived. There were tourists and cars everywhere. The restaurants were full to bursting with people spilling out into the road and music was playing in the distance.

Alyson unhooked my lead once we had crossed all the main roads. The square was in front of us, and I knew exactly what to do. I scampered ahead, racing between the legs of the people milling around, and snaked my way up to the ice cream shop. They had a little counter with a waitress serving customers and I looked up excitedly. *There it is. The ice cream.* The people were waiting in a line. *Ah, I know what that means. Alyson always makes us stand at the back.* I trotted over and sat down behind the last person.

Alyson seemed to take ages to catch up with me, and she was laughing as she approached the kiosk. "There you are. I might have known you'd be here. Trust you to work it all out." She patted me on the head. "Ice cream with two spoons it is then."

It was delicious. I sat transfixed, waiting for each little plastic spoon of creamy yumminess to be placed in front of me. I kept getting drops of ice cream on my nose, which made Alyson giggle. It was all gone too quickly, though, as she scooped up the empty pot and spoons and wiped the table with a serviette.

"No more today, Missy. But we'll come back next weekend." She poured out some water for me and I slurped it noisily, droplets flying into the air as I drank.

We ambled down a side street and Alyson stopped to browse in all the windows of the shops. I was quite happy with that, as it gave me time to sniff everything. One shop sold antiques and 'junk', as Alyson called it, but I loved seeing what they piled up outside. There was a low table with a cage balanced on top and I could hear chirruping and whistling as I approached it. Inside was a brightly coloured bird. Its wings were yellow and green, and it had bright, beady black eyes like little buttons sewn onto its head. It seemed so sad sat there, talking to itself.

I pranced up to it and peered into the cage. The bird shot backwards on its perch, cawing and screeching, scrabbling with its claws to stay attached to the thin sliver of wood it was sitting on. I pushed my nose forward, sniffing. *Urgh!* The cage smelt of poo and burnt paper, and rotting, stale fruit. I wondered how the bird sat there all day surrounded by those horrible scents. It was still scurrying along the perch, squawking, as I walked away.

Next door was a shop selling toys and gifts. Alyson knew the owner and stopped to talk to her outside. *This is more like it.* A basket caught my eye, tucked to one side. It was full of soft fluffy toys. I trotted over. *What a find!* Perched on the top of the pile was a bright blue dolphin cuddly toy. It was irresistible. Alyson was busy chatting as I checked around. *I'm sure she won't mind.* I picked it up carefully, settling my teeth into its soft fur, and sat down, the dolphin still in my mouth.

Alyson turned round, and I wagged my tail, waiting for her to praise me. *Look what I've found!*

"Oh no, I'm so sorry." She spoke to the shop owner and pointed her finger at me. Her eyes narrowed. "What have you got there, you monkey? You're not supposed to pick things up like that."

She reached into her back pocket and pulled out her purse. "I'm sorry. Looks like I am buying a dolphin today. How much do I owe you?" She stepped inside the shop, and I followed her, still carrying my new toy.

"I'm trying to tell you off, young lady. Stop looking so cute with that dolphin sticking out of your mouth. And don't do that again." I could tell Alyson was trying not to laugh, as she stood with her hands on her hips looking down at me.

We walked home, and I carried the dolphin all the way, my head held high. I might not have eaten the ham, but my tummy was full of ice cream and I had a new toy. It had been another good day.

CHAPTER TWENTY-FIVE

Angrinha beach was deserted as we rounded the lifeboat station corner and I padded onto the soft sand. I lifted my head, my nose scenting the air and took a deep breath. A gentle breeze ruffled my feathers. The early morning sun was already warm on my back as I stood with my paws planted on the ground.

I set off, racing across the beach, full of the joy of simply being alive, at one with the nature all around me. The waves bounced and tipped onto the shoreline, leaving shiny trails of water behind them as they slipped back into the sea. The sand glistened, tiny shells nestled amongst the slivers of seaweed that littered the shore, and the seagulls whirled overhead.

Suddenly I stopped, my nose twitching. Alyson was sauntering along, enjoying the scenery far behind me. *I can smell a fish. Where is it?* The high tide line was still visible on the sand in front of the dunes that caressed the beach like giant arms, holding everything in place. I scampered up, my paws slipping as the sand gave way beneath me. It was softer here than near the shoreline, and harder to walk on.

Over there. I ran, head down, nose scouring the ground. The scent was stronger, almost overpowering, as I leapt forward and found the culprit. A giant rotting fish lay on the sand, part buried under a large skein of slimy seaweed. *Perfect.* I lay down, sniffing and gasping with delight, shimmied forward and rolled over onto my back, all four legs in the air, wriggling from side to side. *Heaven.*

Alyson's chuckles filled the air as she approached me. "What are you up to now, you little monkey?" I was still upside down and I grinned at her, waving my legs around and squirming my body further into the fishy carcass.

"Urgh! You stink."

Well, that's charming, isn't it? I righted myself and shook my body; the shimmy reaching down to my tail. Pieces of fish bone and skin flew into the air as Alyson ducked, cupped her arms over her head and squealed.

I trotted along the beach; my head held high. Alyson tried to entice me into the sea, but I was having none of it. *Why would I want to wash away all that fabulous fishy goodness? No chance.*

We walked home, Alyson holding my lead as far away from me as she could and making lots of muttering noises about how smelly I was.

"My eyes are watering Missy, I'm not sure I want to be associated with you today."

We arrived home and Alyson left me in the front garden. "You're not coming inside smelling like that." She came back with my food and water bowl, and I gulped and slurped my breakfast down.

Dave came outside and waved his arms at me, wrinkling his nose and gasping. "Oh good grief, you're right. She stinks. Bath time for you, young lady."

I thought they were both being a bit dramatic, to be honest. It was only a rotting fish, nothing to get that excited about. Dave picked me up and carried me into the bathroom downstairs, plonking me into the shower tray. *Uh-oh.* As soon as Alyson entered the room carrying towels and a bottle of shampoo, I realised what was coming.

I closed my eyes as the warm water cascaded over me, wriggling under Alyson's fingers as she massaged the stinky shampoo into my body. I couldn't see what the problem was. *Surely the nice fishy odour is better than this horrible synthetic stuff being rubbed into my skin? I'm going to stink of apples for days.*

I gave myself a good shake, sending water and shampoo flying everywhere. Alyson squealed. "This isn't even working. I can still smell that fish."

Dave popped his head round the doorway. "I've just looked it up for you. Apparently, tomato sauce is great for getting rid of the stench of fish. We've got a carton of passata somewhere, I'll fetch it, and we'll try that."

He reappeared, and Alyson spread a load of sauce onto my back. *This is getting worse by the minute. I'm going to smell like the casserole Dave cooked for dinner last night.*

She rubbed and scratched, showered and shampooed, until I thought I would be there all day. Finally, she lifted me out, and I shook myself again, glad to be free at last. I covered the far wall of the bathroom with water as Dave dived out of the way and Alyson covered her face with a towel.

Trotting into the lounge, I found my favourite spot on the sofa, which someone had covered with a towel. I settled down to lick my paws and fell asleep dreaming of my lovely smelly fishy friend on the beach.

🐾 🐾 🐾 🐾 🐾

"I think she needs a haircut again." Dave sank down on the sofa beside Alyson.

"I know. But we can't go back to the last place. We'll have to find a new groomer."

I opened my eyes and listened carefully. *That doesn't sound good. I'd better pay attention to this.*

"There's someone advertising on Facebook. She's new to the area, British. Just set up her own place near Guia. Why don't we get in touch with her, see what she's like?"

"Good idea." Dave shuffled along the sofa and stroked me. "Only the best for our girl, though. If she's not happy, we'll have to keep going until we find a groomer she likes."

"I'll call her and see what she says." Alyson went off to the office, and I heard her chatting to someone.

"All sorted. She sounds very nice, and she's used to nervous dogs. She said to bring her in next Tuesday, and she'll take all afternoon if she has to."

A few days later, Alyson walked me out to the car and fastened me into the back seat. I could feel her tension as she drove, and I sensed where we were heading. I sank down in my seat as we parked up in front of a small building.

"Come on, clever clogs. I swear you know where we're going." Alyson hurried me along the pavement, looking for a grassy spot for me to have a wee. A lady came outside and bent down to say hello to me, and I relaxed slightly. She seemed nice, with a soft voice, as we walked inside her shop.

Yes, I was right. A tall table, lots of pulley things hanging from the ceiling, and a metal cage in the corner. In the opposite corner lay an old dog, fast asleep. He was lying on a big blanket and barely raised his head up as I entered the room, then settled down and closed his eyes again.

"Thanks for seeing us, Nicola. She had an awful experience with the last groomer and I'm pretty sure she will not be too happy about this." Alyson hoisted me onto the table and stood cradling me as she talked to the other lady. *Nicola. So that's her name. And she's a groomer. I knew it.*

Nicola stood talking to me, her voice gentle and calm. She set up her machine and raised the table higher. I swayed and lost my footing for a second, but Alyson was there to catch me.

"You can stay right here with her. That's fine with me. And I'll take things slowly. We can stop whenever we need to." Nicola switched on the machine and a low humming sound filled the room. I knew what was coming next as I squirmed around, trying to move out of her reach.

The machine snaked over my back. I flinched, waiting for it to hurt, but it didn't. The metal glided across me as my curls fell to the table. Nicola was talking to me the whole time, and my breathing slowed a little. *That's not so bad.* Alyson was beside me too, whispering into my ear and stroking me.

Soon the table was a mass of black fluffy curls, and the machine stopped whirring.

"Let's take a break, let her have a run around. After that, I'll come back and do her bum and legs."

I was glad of the rest; it was tiring standing there, and I settled outside in a little garden area in the sunshine. Alyson and Nicola sat chatting and drinking coffee. All too soon, it was time for more torture, as Nicola placed me back on the table and trimmed around my bum. I didn't like that part. Then she carried me over to the bathroom. *Another wash? I had one last week. More smelly shampoo for me to extinguish on my next walk. I wonder if I can find another rotting fish to roll in?*

"I don't think I'll try the hairdryer today." Nicola lifted me out of the bathtub and dried me with a fluffy towel. "Let her dry naturally. I'll pop her back on the table for a last once over, then she's done."

I thought we had finished, but she ran the machine all over me again, and trimmed the fur around my paws with some sharp, menacing scissors. Finally, it was all over, and Nicola handed me a big, juicy, meaty biscuit.

I shook myself as soon as I was on the ground, skidding along the floor, trying to get out of the door.

"I think she's had enough. She wants to escape." Alyson fastened my harness and lead on me. "Thank you so much. You've been brilliant and so gentle with her. We'll definitely be back."

Well, I wouldn't go that far with my praise. But it wasn't as bad as that other place. I shuddered as I remembered how brutal that woman had been, her hands gripping me and twisting me around as she carved her cutting machine across my belly. And no horrible cage this time, just a pleasant garden. *It was definitely an improvement.*

There was a cold emptiness across my back where all my warm

curls had disappeared. But it was fresher, too, and my legs moved more easily as I raced around.

"Come on, treat time. We're near a lovely nature reserve. Let's go for a walk, shall we?" Alyson settled me into the car, then only a few minutes later stopped and parked up again. I jumped out, sniffing the air, and followed her as she made her way to a wooden boardwalk. A low bridge straddled a river, and I peeped through the slats on the side as we walked across it. No ducks. But there was something swimming in the water.

"Look, there are turtles down there." Alyson stopped and peered over the railings. The air smelt so fresh, there was a gentle breeze skipping across the water, and the sky was a brilliant shining shade of blue.

The walkway led to a small path that wound its way beside the river, twisting away into the distance. Suddenly Alyson pointed and gasped. "Flamingos. Look at them all over there. They're stunning, so beautiful."

We climbed up some steps to a platform that jutted out over the water. It was so peaceful. Birds were chattering in the trees on the far side of the river, and faint ripples on the water moved in delicate swirls, caught in the sunlight. The reeds swayed, moved by an invisible creature swimming below the surface as I strained forward to see what it was.

"Steady on, don't fall over the edge." Alyson grabbed my harness as I turned around and looked up at her. I wished I could tell her how happy I was at that very moment, surrounded by nature and feeling safe and loved.

"I love you so much, little one." Alyson smothered me in a big hug, and I licked her hand, letting my body relax in her arms. Her eyes were bright as she nuzzled me, dropping kisses onto my nose as I gazed up at her face.

Maybe she knows already.

CHAPTER TWENTY-SIX

"Let's go to Estômbar this afternoon. Kat will love it there."
My ears pricked up. Alyson was talking to Dave as they sat outside in the garden eating their lunch.

"Yes, that's a good idea. I'm sure there are rabbits there. She'll have a field day... literally!"

Rabbits. Did he say rabbits? A quiver of excitement rippled through my body and tickled my tail. *Come on, let's go. Rabbits.* They seemed to take forever finishing their lunch and getting ready, but finally, we were on our way.

I stared out of the window for the entire journey and shot out of the car door when Alyson opened it. I looked around me, but I didn't need to see them. As soon as I lifted my nose, I could smell them. That earthy, flowery, meaty aroma. *Rabbits. And lots of them too.*

I set off, scampering along a narrow path lined with plants and herbs. We turned a corner and in front of us a river glistened in the afternoon sunshine. Trees lined the route, their branches forming a dome of green diffused light to walk under, and everywhere was calm and peaceful.

We passed a picnic area, wooden tables and benches neatly placed in rows, and I snuffled under each one, hoping to find some leftover titbits to scoff. Alyson laughed and called me over to her as she stood by the river, looking across at a group of white birds squabbling in the water. Dave was busy with his camera, setting up his tripod, and we left him to it and walked down to the path by the river.

"This is one of my favourite places in the whole world," Alyson said, as she ambled along, stopping to wait for me as I sniffed and explored every inch of the ground. My nose was in a frenzy, twitching and jerking as I got closer to where I sensed the rabbits had been playing. *Let me at them.*

I raced along, my nose almost touching the ground. *Where are they?* It was so frustrating. Their scent was all around me, but I couldn't find them. It was as if they had vanished.

A hill led away from the path. Small rocks and boulders lined the track, and I thought I saw a slight movement at the top. *Is that an ear sticking out of that bush up there?* I scrambled up the bank, my paws holding firm in the soil as I pushed myself upwards, straining to reach the top. Grass flew up in the air and a back leg disappeared into the undergrowth. *Over there. A rabbit.* I turned and sped off in that direction, then stopped, panting. *Why are they so difficult to catch?*

Alyson whistled to me. I had one last glance around, then headed back down, my paws trudging through the soil. *I'll get you next time.*

The river turned into a wide lake as we reached the end of the path, and I waded into the cool water, enjoying the sensation of it rippling around my legs and paws. The sky overhead was a clear, soft blue, shimmering in the distance and reflecting its light on the water. A large white bird swooped across the surface of the river, diving and emerging with a fish trapped in its beak. Its wings beat rhythmically as it rose upwards, and a whoosh of air tickled my face as it swept past me.

"Wow, did you see that?" Alyson was sitting on the edge of a small wooden jetty, her legs dangling over the side, feet hovering inches above the water. She looked so content and happy as she lifted her head back and smiled, the sun lighting up her face. I padded over to her and lay down, my head resting on my paws. She stroked me, and a wave of contentment rose in my body, its warmth spreading deep inside me. I relaxed and drifted off to sleep, listening to the water lapping gently on the shore.

"Come on, sleepyhead. Time to walk back and find out what your dad has been up to with his camera."

The bright sunlight caught me unawares as I opened my eyes and blinked. I shook my head, trying to dislodge the round ball of white light imprinted inside my brain. I couldn't see the lake in front of me for several seconds until the glimmering flash of light faded. We sauntered along the river path, and I stopped to explore even more of the little offshoots and dead ends that curved their way around the plants and trees. Rabbit droppings were all over the ground, mingled with the scents of other animals and birds, herbs and rich soil.

It was the perfect afternoon, only spoilt by the fact those blasted rabbits had evaded me. Their scent filled my nose as I jumped into the car and vowed to catch one of the little blighters next time.

Another aroma that caused me great excitement each morning was my daily game of 'find the cleaner'. The village had a lady that swept the streets, pushing her plastic cart and broom along as she worked. She kept a bag of dog treats in that cart, and it was my job each day to find her and say hello. Her name was Sandra, but Alyson called her 'Sandra *Bolacha*', as she fed all the stray dogs in the village with her secret stash of dog biscuits.

She had taken a shine to me one day when Alyson stopped to chat to her, and handed me a treat. It became a game then, hunting her down in the narrow back streets each day, and getting my biscuit from her. We would turn a corner and there she was, much to Alyson's surprise, which always made me smile. It was so easy to find Sandra. After all, she was pushing a big smelly plastic bin full of rubbish!

We often saw stray dogs on our walks. Well, most of them were not strays, apparently. They had a home, but their owners opened the door or gate each morning and left them to wander round the village all day. I would say hello to them, then politely trot on. I still wasn't too sure about other dogs and preferred to keep my distance.

One morning down at the beach, we spotted a dog that had obviously been abandoned. The poor thing was huddled up beside the fishermen's huts behind the beach. As soon as it saw us, it was off like a bullet fired from a gun, scarpering off along the path, tail hung low between its legs.

It was several days later before we noticed it again. This time Alyson got close enough to realise it was a young boy, and a terribly skinny and unwell boy at that. He wasn't much more than a puppy really, as he stood there shivering and whimpering at us. I walked forward tentatively, sniffing the air to find out more about him, but all I could smell was his fear, which was wrapped around him like a damp cloak. He was plotting his escape route, and I tried to reassure him, dropping my head low and wagging my tail.

He crept forward slowly, grabbed the biscuit Alyson had placed on the ground, then shot away to hide behind the huts again. It was so sad to watch. I remembered how scared I had been, scavenging for food on the streets, fearful of every person who approached me, expecting them to hurt me. I had been hit and kicked many times. That low body stance, head down, eyes darting from side to side, tail quivering nervously. Those signs were so familiar to me.

The next morning we saw Dagmar with her dogs and Alyson mentioned the stray pup to her. She promised to keep an eye out for him, and over the coming weeks, we often spotted him hiding behind the huts, cowering and trembling if anyone went near him. Eventually Dagmar gained his trust and fed him each day, but it was several more weeks before he ventured close enough for her to touch him.

Alyson asked her what she was going to do with him.

"I'm not sure. I've already got six dogs. But I can't leave him here." Dagmar swept her hand across her eyes and sighed. "I've found out his story, though. He belonged to a German couple with a camper van. They spent the winter here, then packed up one morning and just drove away, leaving him behind. The poor dog won't leave the beach in case they come back for him."

It was such a sad story. Dagmar had named him Sandy, and he came trotting over to her now when she called him and hovered nearby. He was still shaking, eyes wide and alert. I could tell he was likely to run at any moment, but his hunger overcame his fears as he sat waiting to be fed.

It took many more weeks before Dagmar coaxed him closer, until one day she slipped a collar over his head and attached a lead to him. The next time we saw him, he was a different dog. He held his head high as he trotted along with the rest of the pack, tail wagging.

"Looks like you've got seven now, then?" Alyson asked Dagmar, as she smiled over at Sandy.

"Yes, I know. I can hardly afford to look after the six I already have, but I couldn't leave him here. He's actually a very gentle dog, and he's fine with the others. So seven it is. But no more. He's the last."

I was glad to know he had found a home with someone that would love him and take care of him, and I gave Alyson an extra lick on her hand that morning when she fed me. I hoped she knew how much she had changed my life the day she adopted me, and that I would be forever grateful to her.

CHAPTER TWENTY-SEVEN

My lunchtime and night walks with Alyson were often just quick strolls around our local neighbourhood for me to do my business. I am always very particular about where I go, especially for a wee, and often take several minutes selecting exactly the right spot. Alyson guffawed with laughter the first time she watched me hoist my leg up in the air.

"Most girl doggies crouch down, you know."

That bemused me. I found it much easier to lift my leg up. It helped when I was trying to reach a spot high on a wall that had already been marked by another dog. Alyson called it my 'top trumps' game, but luckily she didn't seem to mind waiting while I sniffed and processed every scent along the road.

She didn't let me sniff everything, though. I was minding my own business (literally!) one afternoon when she suddenly yanked hold of my lead and spun me backwards. I almost fell over.

"Eek, get away from them!"

I hadn't a clue what she was shouting about, as I looked down at the ground. On the pavement, right in front of me, was a row of fluffy caterpillars wriggling along in a line. They were almost joined from head to toe; they were so close together. It was like a long train of fluffy wriggling worms, and they were obviously in a hurry. I was desperate to have a closer look.

"No, no, don't touch them. They're poisonous. Come away, quick."

Alyson dragged me down the road, my back legs flailing as we raced away. Finally we stopped, and she leant forward, hands on knees, her breath coming in quick gasps.

"Phew, that was lucky. I'm glad I spotted them before you did. They're really dangerous to dogs, and humans too."

They just looked like little cute caterpillars to me, and I couldn't see anything wrong with them, but Alyson stared up the road. Her eyes narrowed and her eyebrows dipped down. I knew that look.

"Right, we'll have to avoid that route for a while. There's a pine tree on the corner, that's obviously where they're coming from."

I bowed my head. That was my favourite night-time location. I loved going for a wee in the grass beside that tree.

Sure enough, that night we turned up a different road and Alyson kept me on a lead. We sauntered past a row of houses, then down a side road, heading home. It was much darker, and Alyson tightened her grip on my lead. Not all the streetlights were working, but that didn't bother me as I snuffled along the road, weaving between the parked cars and the pavement.

Suddenly, I stiffened, the hairs on the back of my neck standing to attention. Something was under the car beside me. I tentatively stuck my nose underneath and sniffed.

Ouch! I shot backwards and yelped.

A claw appeared from beneath the car, bristling with talons extended. A sharp yowl pierced the air as a cat emerged, spitting and snarling.

I shot forward, barking. Usually that was enough to frighten a cat, and I growled and waited for it to turn tail and run away.

It spat at me again, its paw extended, then pounced forward, knocking into me. Something sharp scratched me above my eye and I instinctively put my paw up to check my face. That left me off balance, as the cat whipped around and crashed into me. Its hot breath swilled over me as spittle showered my face. I whimpered as its claws scratched my neck.

Alyson screamed and tried to pull me away from the cat. Instead of retreating, it came at us again, as Alyson dropped my lead and stepped in front of me, blocking my view. The cat yowled and launched itself at Alyson, scratching and biting her leg. It was late summer, and she was only wearing a T-shirt and shorts, leaving her legs exposed.

"Get away from me, you little shit." Alyson kicked out, trying to frighten the cat, as it spun around and attacked her again. I shoved past her, growling and barking, my head whirling. I tasted blood as a flash of red hit my eyes. *Is that my blood?* I ducked around Alyson. She was kneeling down, her leg bleeding as she cradled her ankle in her hands.

The cat dived back under the car, only to emerge from the other side with another cat. This one was much larger. Its back was curled upwards in an arch, teeth bared. *Oh no, there are two of them.* I braced myself, planting my feet firmly, standing in front of Alyson. *If they're going to hurt my mom again, they'll have to get past me to do it.* I barked, shaking with fear, but determined they would not see how scared I was. *They are just cats. They're supposed to run away from me. What's going on?*

Alyson recovered and stood up, shouting at them to go away. She aimed a kick at the first cat and I launched forward, snarling and growling. The cat stepped back, and I barked again as it slunk away. That only left the second cat, who was creeping towards Alyson. It shot out a paw, scratching her leg as she cried out.

It was too dark to see everything that was happening, and the cat moved so swiftly. Alyson spun around, shouting and waving her arms in the air and I continued barking, until finally the second cat scurried off. The road was empty ahead and Alyson grabbed my lead and set off at a fast pace. I was happy to run alongside her. My head was pounding, and I couldn't see clearly out of one eye. Heroics could wait for another day. I was just glad to escape.

We arrived home and Alyson dropped to her knees in front of me.

"My poor baby, are you hurt?" She swept her fingers all over me, pausing over my face, her hand trembling slightly. "We are in a bit of a mess, aren't we?" She gazed at her leg. Blood was trickling down her shin. She wiped it away and shook her head.

"Never mind about me. I'll be alright. Let's get you inside and clean you up first."

I trotted into the kitchen and waited as Alyson put towels on the floor and wiped a damp flannel over my eyes and face. She peered at me, her eyes scrunched up.

"You're okay. Just a scratch. But it's so close to your eye." She wiped her fingers across her forehead, her hand shaking. "If it had been a few millimetres lower. That doesn't bear thinking about."

Dave arrived home a few minutes later. He'd been away on a photo shoot, and gasped when he saw us in the kitchen, towels covered in blood on the floor.

"What on earth? Are you alright? Is Missy hurt?" He dropped his bags and rushed over to us.

"Oh my god, what happened to you?" He picked up a towel and looked at Alyson's leg. "Get cleaned up and I'll sort out in here. Is Kat okay?"

"Yes, she's fine. I checked her all over. It was a cat. Well, two cats. They came from nowhere. We walked past a car, and they must have been hiding underneath. Next thing I knew, they were attacking Kat. She took a swipe on the face, but luckily it missed her eye." Alyson's hands were still shaking.

"The little sods came at me twice. Kat tried to save me, she got in between me and the first cat. It all happened so quickly, and it was pretty dark, too. I could feel the blood dripping down my leg, but I was more worried about Kat than anything else. I couldn't see what had happened until we got back home."

"Why did they attack you like that?" Dave stroked my head, his touch gentle as he caressed me.

"I don't know. Maybe they had a litter under the car they were trying to protect. Who knows? I've never seen a cat react like that before. And then a second one appeared and started attacking us as well. I can't believe no-one heard us from the houses nearby. I was screaming and Kat was barking so loudly, it's a wonder someone didn't come outside."

Dave pointed at Alyson's leg. "I think you'd better go to the health centre tomorrow and have it looked at." He soaked a cloth in warm water and cleaned her leg as Alyson winced. "If they are stray cats, you'll probably need a tetanus jab. Just to be on the safe side."

"Great. Just what I need." Alyson touched my head. "Thank goodness Missy here is alright. That scratch is awfully close to her eye. She was so brave, protecting me. You're such a darling girl. I love you so much." She bent over and kissed me.

"I'll find a different route tomorrow night. I only went that way because of the pine tree and the processionary caterpillars." She sighed. "So much for protecting us from one thing. I led us straight into another problem."

"You weren't to know the cats were under that car. You're right; they must have been protecting a litter or something for them to react like that. At least there's no serious harm done. And well done Kat for protecting your mommy. I think that calls for a slice of ham, don't you?"

I wagged my tail. *Now you're talking.*

The next day Alyson went to the health centre and returned with her leg bandaged.

"You were right," she said to Dave, dropping her purse and keys on the table. "I had to have a tetanus jab. My arm's a bit sore. And they've given me antibiotics. You won't believe it, though. My appointment only cost four euros and fifty cents, and that included the tetanus shot. And the prescription was less than four euros. Amazing."

"Well, that's good news. At least it didn't cost a lot. And it could have been much worse. I think you both got off lightly." Dave patted me on the head. "Good job Kat was there looking after you."

I fell asleep, feeling proud of my little family. I hoped they knew I would always protect them. And the slices of ham afterwards were a definite bonus too.

CHAPTER TWENTY-EIGHT

Alyson and Dave were eating their dinner, and I sat on my bed beside the table. I knew I was not allowed to beg for food, even though their meals always smelt fantastic. Alyson had explained to me it was because they wanted to take me everywhere with them, including when they ate at a café or restaurant. I had to sit quietly beside them or under the table if it was a busy place, but I didn't mind that. I just enjoyed being with them. Going out was always exciting.

One day we drove to the top of the world to see the view. It was a long way, but Alyson and Dave were in high spirits.

"I love Fóia," Dave said, "but let's stop off in Monchique en route. We've got time for an ice cream and a wander." He parked up, and we walked up a cobbled street that led to a wide square, surrounded by shops and houses.

I'd never been there before, and I happily circled around, sniffing and exploring. There were some people in the distance. One boy stood with his arm in the air, a bird perched on his hand. Two more figures were sitting on concrete blocks and a boy sat on the pavement, his legs stretched wide apart.

As I got closer, I sniffed the air. *That's strange. They look like people, but they don't smell right. And they're not moving.* I sidled up to the boy sat on the floor, and hesitated. *Why doesn't he say something?*

Alyson knelt beside me and patted the boy's head. "They're statues, Kat. They're not real."

I sniffed him tentatively. He smelt of metal, dog wee, and bird poo. It was most odd. I checked out the boy standing still. Even the bird on his hand wasn't real. I walked round all four statues, trying to make sense of it all.

"Come on, let's get an ice cream."

Yes please. I trotted after Dave, glancing behind me one more time at the statues. They were very odd. I shook my head. *Humans are a strange lot.*

After a few slurps of delicious fluffy ice cream, we jumped back in the car and drove up a steep, winding road. It was narrow in places, and Alyson was a bit scared. I could tell that by the way her hand was gripping the door handle, and the funny squeaking noise she made on one of the bends.

We pulled up in a car park and I hopped out, eager to explore. The wind whirled around us, pulling me into its embrace as it swept over me. The sky was enormous here, full of fluffy white clouds scudding across the dome of blue stretched above us. We were so high up the sky was closer to me than the sea far below. The view was amazing, rocks and hills merging into a pattern of brown and green, swirling and dancing before us. I gulped as I peered over the edge of a boulder. There was nothing below us for miles except grassland and fields. Way down in the distance, the sea sparkled and shimmered. It was exciting, but scary too, and I stayed close to Alyson. Just in case she needed my help, of course.

We strolled around, and I sniffed every rock, fascinated by the scents of all the different animals and birds that had left their marks. There were piles of pebbles stacked in little mounds and pillars. Some were almost as tall as me. I nudged one pebble with my nose and it fell off, tumbling down the hillside as Alyson laughed at me.

"Right, time to visit Paul and Sandra. I think their son, Matthew, will be there, too. He's over from the UK, staying with them for a couple of weeks." Dave gathered up his camera, and we headed back to the car.

"That'll be nice. We haven't seen them in ages. And they haven't met Kat yet."

We drove a short way down the hill, then parked up and I jumped out of the car. I could smell chicken roasting and I lifted my nose up, breathing in the aromas wafting across the road.

"We're going there later, Missy." Alyson pointed to the restaurant opposite. "But first, come and meet our friends."

I trotted after her as we made our way through an enormous gate and entered a lush garden. There was a swimming pool and a traditional house nestled into the grounds. The view was almost as good as the one we had left behind at the top of the mountain. The sea was far beneath us in the distance, way below the sweeping pattern of the hills.

Three people came over to say hello, and I let them fuss over me, hoping they might have doggy treats hidden in their pockets. Everyone sat around an enormous table outside and I settled down beside Alyson as she gave me some water and biscuits.

They seemed to chat for ages and I fell asleep, only stirring when Alyson fastened my lead onto my collar.

"Come on, Kat, time for dinner."

We walked over the road to the restaurant. It was late autumn and quiet outside as we trooped up the steps, and I gasped as Dave opened the door and stepped inside. The others followed, and I panicked. *Are they going to leave me outside?* I didn't fancy that very much.

"It's alright, we asked the waitress. You can come in with us," Alyson said to me. "But you must sit quietly under the table, okay?"

I followed her inside. There were a couple of people sitting at a table near the door, but they didn't even glance up as I walked past them. Alyson tucked me in beside her under an empty chair in the corner and I lay down, peeking my nose out so that I could see into the room.

Soon, their table was full of food. It smelt delicious. My mouth was watering, but all I got were a few little doggy treats that Alyson slipped down to me. It was quite boring after the initial excitement of being inside a restaurant had worn off. They were all chatting and laughing as I fell asleep, my head tucked on my paws.

Alyson scraped back her chair and stood up. I woke with a start. *Where am I?* I looked out of the window, but it was dark outside. *How long have I been asleep?*

"You've been brilliant, young lady. Not a peep out of you all night. Good girl."

The restaurant was now full of people, all talking and eating. The smells were amazing. Roast chicken, chips, and tempting fishy odours assailed my nose as I stood up and sniffed the air.

"Come on, time to go."

Blast. I was hoping to have a nosey under the tables, in case anyone had dropped any food on the floor. *Finders, keepers, and all that. No chance.* Alyson escorted me swiftly towards the door, and I heard several people gasp. A knife clattered onto a plate and it all went quiet, as someone exclaimed, "A dog! Where did that come from?"

"Wow, did you have a dog sat beside you?" a lady asked Alyson.

"Yes, but she's very good. She's no trouble at all."

"I can't believe it. What an amazing dog. Fancy hiding her away under the table. Incredible."

Alyson smiled at the waitress and thanked her as we left the restaurant.

"You can come back anytime with her. She was so good tonight. No-one even knew she was there." I stopped to let the waitress pat my head, then walked out to the car, feeling quite proud of myself.

Wintertime was fast approaching, and Alyson explained we were going to an event that signalled the start of Christmas. I didn't really know what that meant, but I was always happy to tag along wherever they were going. We went to Lagoa, and Dave drove round looking for somewhere to park. There were cars abandoned everywhere.

"This will have to do. We'll have to walk from here."

We set off through the town and eventually reached one of the main streets. There was a line of red carpet-like material stretched across the pavement. A path of red spread out into the distance, and I stopped to sniff it. *Hey, this would be a glorious spot for a wee.* Before I could even lift my leg up, Alyson had dragged me away.

"No, not here. You can't go here."

She's reading my mind again.

We walked a bit further, and I found a little tree tucked away down a lane. *Perfect.* We returned to the carpet road, and I stopped dead. There, in front of me, was one of those statue things. It was a man, dressed head to toe in what looked like tinfoil, stood perfectly still, holding out his hand.

Ah-ha! I'm not falling for that trick again. I know you're not real. I stepped forward, sniffing the air. *That's funny. He smells real. Must be all these other people milling around, putting me off the scent.*

I stopped beside the silver man and stared up at him intently. *Hang on a minute. Did he just wink at me?* I shook my head. *I must be imagining things.*

Suddenly, his arm shot upwards and waved at the crowd. I leapt up and barked. *He's real!* I spun around, then looked back at him. He was laughing as he leant forward and patted me on the head.

"You weren't expecting that, were you?" Dave was laughing too as Alyson bent down and hugged me. "Oh Kat, that was funny. Did you think he was a statue like the ones in Monchique? These are different. They're living statues. Real people standing still." We walked off, Alyson and Dave still chuckling to themselves.

There were statues everywhere, with people standing watching them. There was a green man sitting on a bicycle that seemed to float in the air. His legs were pedalling round and round, but he wasn't moving anywhere. He tipped his hat to me as I sat in front of him. I liked bicycle man. He was nice and smiley.

We wandered round the streets looking at all the statues. I was still a little bemused by it all, but everyone seemed to be enjoying themselves. Dave was in his element with his camera, pausing to take photos of everything. Alyson rolled her eyes at him and left him to it, stopping at a café to have a drink. I sat beside her, grateful for the water and dog food she gave me. Statue watching was thirsty work.

We returned to the green man again. He was definitely my favourite. The fairies perched on the branches of a tree had frightened me. I didn't realise they were there until I looked up and saw their faces peering down at me, but I liked the green man. He waved at me as Dave joined us and took some more photos of the magical bicycle man.

"Finally! I wondered where you'd got to. Right, time to find the car then and go home. I'm starving." Alyson gathered up her things.

"I think it's somewhere up there," Dave said, pointing over his shoulder. "But I'm not exactly sure. We don't normally park that far out. We'd better go back the way we came. I'm sure it's a longer way round, but at least we know the route."

I listened to them. *So we need to go back to the car? Well, that's easy. It's the way you pointed to a minute ago.* I started off in that direction, then came to a halt as Alyson pulled me back on my lead.

"Hang on, Missy. Not that way. We need to find the car."

I know. It's this way.

"She thinks we parked over there," Alyson said to Dave.

"Well, you can go that way. Don't blame me if you get lost, though. I'm going the way I know. And there's a shop I want to pop into beside the market."

"Well, okay, I'm going to trust Kat. She seems to know which way to go and my feet are hurting. A shortcut would be great."

"I'll see you back at the car then." Dave walked away, then swivelled round. "Bet I get there before you."

"No chance," Alyson muttered as she set off with me. "Come on, Missy. Show me what you're made of. Find our car."

We set off up the road and I turned sharp right at a road junction and headed off into the small streets surrounding the shops. The pavements were narrower here, the houses almost tipping over into the road, as we tramped along the *calçada* cobbles.

We came to a junction, and I stopped for a second to sniff the air and get my bearings.

"I hope you know where the car is, Kat. Because I haven't got a clue. We'd better not be lost."

Lost? No chance. I knew exactly where Dave had parked the car. I just needed to work out the quickest route. Alyson held onto my lead as we crossed a road and rounded the corner. There in front of us was our car. I trotted up to it and shook myself. *That was fun.*

"You're a clever girl. And we beat Dad. Perfect." Alyson settled me on the back seat and gave me a biscuit and some water, then sat in the front passenger seat. She kept looking back at me and smiling.

Dave came trudging up the hill carrying his camera bag. He stopped when he looked into the car and saw us sitting there. A big grin spread across Alyson's face.

"Well, I'll be... How long have you been here?" Dave scratched his head and peered into the car.

"Oh, a good ten minutes. Kat led me straight here. It was incredible. I hadn't a clue where we were, but she knew exactly where she was going."

I settled down and made myself comfortable for the journey home, snorting quietly to myself. *Of course I knew the way to the car. I don't know why they doubted me.* Although I had to admit those living statues had caught me out.

CHAPTER TWENTY-NINE

"I love you with all your soft fluffy curls, Ratty. But spring is almost here, and you need a trim now, before it gets warmer. And you are a bit matted under your tummy." I rolled over onto my back as Alyson stroked me, her fingers tickling my stomach. I looked up at her and sighed. *Back to the groomer then. Not my favourite place. Oh well. At least the treats are always good there.*

I had lots of names now. Most of them were from Alyson as she smothered me in kisses and hugs. She told me she loved me every day, and I don't think she realised how much her words warmed my heart. I still recalled those days spent tied up at the farm and later wandering lost and alone around the villages, but those memories were fading now. Replaced by an ever-increasing collection of new and wonderful experiences and moments of pure love that caressed my soul and made me feel complete.

'Ratty' was one of her favourite names for me. I think it evolved from Kat, which became 'Rat-a-Kat' and finally 'Ratty', but I can't really be sure. 'Monkey' and 'Monkey-bum' were common too, alongside 'Pickle' and 'Poppet'. Oh, and 'Missy' too, of course. It was a wonder I wasn't confused by all those names, but I didn't really mind what I was called. I could tell by the tone of their voice when they were talking to me, or when I had done something wrong. Luckily, the latter happened infrequently. I absolutely hated being naughty or upsetting Alyson or Dave and I was a quick learner, too. If I messed up, they corrected me gently, without shouting at me, and I stored away the information and made sure I didn't make the same mistake twice.

I liked nothing better than being able to please my mom and dad. Seeing the love in their eyes for me and hearing their soft voices as they stroked me or tucked me up at bedtime meant the world to me. I had finally stopped worrying they might abandon me or leave me. They were my family. Alyson often said to me, "I will always love you, and always be your mommy. Forever." She usually accompanied that with an enormous cuddle and lots of kisses on the top of my nose. I had never felt happier.

The groomer's shop was quiet as we arrived and I traipsed inside, hoping that they were closing, and I could escape the torture. *No such luck.* Nicola came bounding out into the reception. She grabbed my lead, and I trudged after her, dragging my paws along the ground.

"Come on, Kat. I won't hurt you." She lifted me onto the table as Alyson stood beside me. I closed my eyes and tried to imagine I was somewhere else as the relentless drone of the trimming machine filled my ears. It seemed like an age before Nicola finished and took me off for a hose down and shampoo. Then it was back to the table, wrapped in a nice fluffy towel.

A horrible noise started up behind me. It sounded like a hundred people all talking at the same time. I shot my head round, eyes wide, ready to snarl at whatever it was.

"It's okay. It's a hairdryer. I'll start it slowly over you. Look, here it is. Nothing to worry about."

It was a monster, shooting hot air at me and whining. I didn't like it at all. I bowed my head, longing for it to be over so I could jump off the table.

"She's got a small lump here," Nicola said as she smoothed her hand along my back.

"I know. We mentioned it to the vet about two years ago, but they said it was just a fatty lump and to monitor it. The next year, another vet even joked about it, saying Kat was a little overweight, and it was extra fat. I thought it had got bigger, but I couldn't really decide through all her fluffy fur and winter curls. I can see it better now." Alyson touched my back, and I winced. *Ouch. That's sore.*

"Oh god, what am I going to do?" I could hear a catch in Alyson's voice.

"Well, it's probably nothing. But I'd get it checked out. Maybe go to a different vet. Just to be on the safe side." Nicola was sweeping all my fur off the table with her hand, having mercifully switched off the hairdryer.

"I'll do that. Thanks again for a great job. Doesn't she look different now, without all that fur? I can see her beautiful eyes again." Alyson looked down at me and I saw a flicker pass across her eyes. *She's worried about something.*

I listened carefully as she chatted with Dave that evening. We were all sitting on the sofa, Alyson stroking me almost absentmindedly as she talked.

"That lump on her back is definitely bigger. Nicola said we should get it looked at, just in case. The problem is, I don't think much of the vet's we've been going to for her annual jabs."

"What happened to the bloke that was there? The one Ginie recommended?" Dave asked.

"He's gone. He works at his other practice now. But that's miles away. The other side of Faro, I think. I'll have to find someone nearer."

We went to bed that night, and Alyson fell asleep with her hand resting on one of my back legs.

The next morning, Marie and her two dogs were at the beach. Alyson stood chatting to her as I scampered around. "Kat's got a lump on her back. I need to get it checked out. You wouldn't know of a good vet locally, would you?"

"Oh yes. Go to ours. Millie had a lump on her leg, and they were brilliant. She was in and out the same day. They removed it, and she healed in no time. It's in Portimão, near the bridge. They're a vet hospital, and they do everything on site."

"Thanks, that's brilliant. I'm so worried about it. I'll call them today." Alyson jotted down the details on her phone, and I trotted up, pretending I hadn't been listening to them.

"Don't worry. She'll be fine. I'm sure it's nothing to worry about. Dogs get lumps all the time. Let me know how it goes, won't you?" Marie patted Alyson's arm and then walked off, whistling at her dogs to follow her.

We went home, and I overheard parts of Alyson's conversation as she talked on her phone. She came into the kitchen and updated Dave.

"They said to bring her in tomorrow morning and they'll have a look at her. They said they'd take a sample and analyse it. And that I wasn't to worry. The receptionist sounded very efficient, and Marie recommended them, so we'll have to wait and see what happens."

"I'm sure Kat will be alright. She's a tough old girl."

Hey, less of the old. Although to be fair, no-one knew how old I was. I tried to work it out once, but all the months and years seemed to merge into one when I was at the farm. I knew how many litters I'd had, but that was about it. *Ginie's vet thought I was about five years old when he first saw me. That would make me about eight and a half now. That's not old.*

The next morning, we all jumped in the car and drove over to Portimão. Dave parked up in front of a big shiny glass-fronted building, and I hesitated at the entrance. I didn't like the smell of the place, even from the outside. As soon as Alyson opened the front door, I recoiled backwards. The stench of chemicals mixed with dog wee and something else metallic and sinister hit my nostrils. It was overpowering. Horrible.

Dave had to drag me inside, and I sat on the floor, shivering. *This isn't a nice place.* A woman in a white coat came out to greet us and showed us into a tiny room. She bent down to pat me while they talked, but she smelt funny. The same chemical aroma in the building clung to her clothes and shoes.

She picked up my lead and walked towards another door at the rear. I looked back at Alyson, who gulped and nodded to me. "It's okay, go with the nice lady. I'll wait here for you."

The door opened, and I peered into the room. It was very busy. People were bustling around, some of them carrying folders and strange objects. There was another room off to the left, full of cages stacked high along the walls. A few dogs were lying inside them, looking out at me or sleeping. The noise wasn't too bad, but it was the smell that made me hesitate. The metal aroma that hung in the air was like a fog floating across my nose and I sneezed, trying to shake off a feeling of foreboding.

"Come on, up here," the lady said as she laid me down on a table. A sharp icy sting pierced my back, and I yelped. "It's alright, almost done. There you go." She stroked my ears, which were lying flat against my head, as I kept looking down. *I don't like this place at all. I want to go home.*

She placed me on the floor, and I skidded in my haste to escape.

"Hang on, little one. Let me get the door open for you first."

I shot through the door as soon as it slid open and raced over to Alyson, feeling her warmth as she held me close in her arms. *Home. Take me home.*

"I'll have the results in a few days for you. Don't worry, I'm sure she'll be fine. I'll get the reception to call you as soon as we know something." White coat lady smiled down at me, but I didn't care. I just wanted to leave.

"Thanks ever so much. Right, come on, Missy. Let's go home."

Finally! I had to wait in the reception area while Alyson paid them some money. Then the front door was open, and I shot outside, gasping as I gulped in the fresh air. I shuddered. *I hope I don't have to go there again.*

Alyson and Dave seemed different once we got home. I received even more cuddles and attention than normal and Alyson was almost glued to my side. She kept staring down at me and telling me how much she loved me, as her eyes filled with tears.

"Look at me, what a mess I am," she said, laughing. But her laughter sounded hollow somehow, and her smile was lopsided and didn't reach her eyes like it normally did. "I'm sure you're going to be fine, and I'm worrying about nothing." She leant over and kissed me on the end of my nose, and I curled up beside her.

CHAPTER THIRTY

A few days later, the phone rang, and I trotted closer as Alyson answered it. I could only hear her side of the conversation, and her shoulders sagged as she sank down onto the sofa opposite me.

"I see. So what does that mean?"

More silence as she listened to the answer.

"Okay. Well, if you think we need to do that. Yes, of course we can come in. When's the next day she's there?"

"That's Easter Sunday? Are you sure? Isn't that a holiday?"

"Okay, that's fine. See you on Sunday."

She put the phone down and Dave came into the lounge.

"Was that the vet's?"

"Yes. They want us to come in and talk to the vet in person. That can't be good, can it? Surely, if it was good news, they would have just told me on the phone?"

Alyson's voice broke. Dave reached over and held her hand.

"So, when do we need to go in?"

"Sunday. Easter Sunday. That's the next day our vet is working, apparently. She wants to see us herself, with Kat."

"Well, it's Friday today. So not long to wait. Try not to worry, love. I'm sure it's nothing. She probably likes to talk to people in person."

I definitely detected that something was wrong. It might have been all the extra juicy succulent chicken pieces that found their way into my food bowl. Or the extended walk along Praia Grande beach the next morning. And the impressive number of cuddles and kisses I had that smothered me. Alyson slept cuddling up to me all night, and I lay there basking in her love and attention. I decided that whatever was up, if it meant I received even more of her time and affection, it couldn't be a bad thing.

We drove to Portimão, and I sighed as we pulled up outside the same building. *Here we go again.* I held my breath as we walked through the front door, but the same horrible smells assaulted me.

The lady in the white coat led us into the little room, and I braced myself for what was about to happen. Instead, I simply sat on the floor and listened as they all talked over the top of my head.

"So, we're not one hundred per cent sure what it is. The lump has some signs of pre-cancerous growth. We won't know for certain unless we remove it."

"So, she needs an operation?"

"Yes, that's my recommendation. We could leave it, but it will continue to grow, which may cause her some discomfort. And there's a risk it might be cancer. I think we need to remove it."

"What will that involve?" Alyson's voice was very quiet as she reached down and stroked me.

"It's a simple procedure. She can be in and out the same day, all being well. We check everything before we start, to make certain she's strong and fit enough for the surgery, so there's no need to worry. If we get time once I've removed the lump, I'll clean her teeth for you as well while she's under the anaesthetic. I noticed they could do with a clean when I saw her the other day."

"If you think we need to remove it, then, of course, we should. When can you do the surgery? We really don't want to wait longer than we have to."

"I'll schedule it for this Tuesday. Pop over to the reception and we'll get it all booked in. And don't worry, she'll be fine. I'll look after her."

Alyson's voice wavered. "Please do. She means the world to us. She's a very special little girl."

"I know. I'm sure she is. I'll take good care of her."

We trooped out to the reception, Alyson signed something, then we drove home. I could almost reach out and touch the silence in the car. As soon as Dave opened the front door, Alyson raced into the bathroom and I could hear her crying. I trotted over to her when she emerged. She was wiping her eyes with a towel and I nuzzled into her. *It's okay. I don't know what's wrong. But please don't cry.*

I licked her face as she smiled at me. "I love you so much, Missy."

That day and the next brought more delicious cooked chicken and even some fresh salmon in my food bowl. We went for long walks on the beach and curled up on the sofa each evening, Alyson's arm draped around me.

At night Alyson spent ages telling me how much she loved me and how special I was. It was very nice, but I could tell something was worrying her underneath her words. Her hand shook slightly as she stroked me, and she had a faraway look in her eyes.

After a shorter than normal walk on the Tuesday morning, Alyson put down a bowl of water for my breakfast. *Where's my food?*

"Sorry, love, you can't eat anything this morning."

I knew something was amiss. My morning bowl of moist, yummy dog food and biscuits was always there. I lapped up the water, then sat with my head on one side, as Alyson sat at the table, toying with her bowl of cereal. *So she's not eating any breakfast either?* It was turning into a strange morning.

"Are you sure you don't want me to come with you? I could delay the photo shoot? Robin has loaned me his car, but I don't have to go today if you don't want me to." Dave was busy in the office, sorting out his camera bags as he shouted over to Alyson.

"No, that's okay. I can drop her off. You might as well do the shoot, there's no point both of us moping around. At least that way you'll be home later this afternoon. I'm going to try to keep busy all day. I can't sit around waiting to hear from them. I'll go mad."

"As long as you're sure. I'd better get going then, and so had you. You have to be there by eight thirty, don't you?"

"Yes, I'll be off in a minute. I'll just finish my cup of tea. I can't eat a thing this morning."

Dave came over and hugged her. "It's all going to be alright. She'll be back home again this evening, right as rain." He bent down and kissed me. "You be a good girl now, Kat. I love you." He moved away quickly, but I saw a glimpse of his eyes before he left the room. *What is it with these guys? They keep crying.*

Alyson grabbed my lead, and I jumped into the back of the car. She drove to Portimão, and I recognised the route over the bridge as I looked out of the window. I was beginning to hate the place, as we parked up and walked to the vet's again. We immediately went into the same little room. I wondered if the lady in the white coat actually lived in there, as she greeted us and Alyson sat down. I stood by the door, wary of what was happening as Alyson signed some forms and patted me on the head.

"Okay baby. Be good now and be brave. I'll be here later to collect you. I love you so much." Her voice caught in her throat as she bent down to kiss me and a tear plopped onto my nose.

White coat lady attached a lead to my collar and walked me to the far door. I looked back at Alyson. She was sitting holding my lead in her hands, winding the fabric around her fingers, her eyes glistening as she nodded at me.

"It's okay. Go with the lady. I'll be here waiting for you. I love you."

The door closed behind us as the lady took me into another small room. She laid me down on a metal table. I felt a sharp prick on my shoulder as something warm seeped down into my body, then everything went dark.

CHAPTER THIRTY-ONE

Alyson tells the next part of this story better than me. Apparently, she sat in the driver's seat of our car, crying for ages. Then she shook herself and went to a local café for some breakfast, but only ate half her ham and cheese croissant. That was most unlike her!

Her plan was to do the weekly shop at the local supermarket to keep herself occupied. She stood at the trolley bay about to enter the store when her phone rang. She looked at the caller ID and it was the vet's. Her heart leapt into her mouth and she gasped. It was only ten thirty. Her first thought was surely it couldn't be good news if they were ringing her that early?

They were quick to reassure her.

"The surgery is over. It went well. Kat's fine, she's sleeping," they said. "You can pick her up at four thirty today."

Alyson admitted she broke down and blubbed in front of all the trolleys and shoppers. The sheer relief of knowing I was alright was too much for her to contain. She said she wanted to run straight over to the vet's and hold me in her arms. She counted how many hours she had to wait until she could bring me home and admitted it was the longest day of her life.

Meanwhile, I woke up and tried to get my bearings as I checked myself over. My head was spinning, my body hurt, and my mouth was sore. There was a tinny metal tang at the back of my throat and when I tried to move, I winced. I turned slowly to find I had a giant plaster stuck to my back. No wonder it felt strange. My paws were cold, my claws clattering on the metal floor of the cage below me. I huddled up and tried to sleep, the noise of the other dogs around me fading into the darkness as my eyes closed.

I heard a woman speaking. The muffled voice swirled in my head, like a soft mist enveloping me. *Am I dreaming? Is someone there? Why do I recognise that voice?*

I opened my eyes, and there was Marie, the lady from the beach. She was staring down at me, her fingers squished between the bars of the cage, reaching out to me. *It must be a dream. How can she be in here?*

"Hello, Kat. I've come over to say hello to you." She stroked one of my paws. "You're going to be fine. And the vet told me you can go home later today. Your mommy will be here to collect you soon."

I was still groggy, my head stuffed full of cotton wool, but her voice and touch were soothing, and I fell asleep.

Alyson told me later it was just a strange coincidence that brought Marie to the vet's that day. Millie, one of her own dogs, was in there the previous day for a minor operation, and they had kept her in overnight. Marie was visiting Millie and came over to find me to give me some fuss and attention.

Marie then drove to our house to tell Alyson what she had done and to reassure her I looked well and I was sleeping. I know that meant a lot to Alyson.

A nurse woke me later that afternoon and lifted me out of the cage. My legs wobbled as I placed my paws on the ground and took a couple of hesitant steps. *That's not too bad.* I shook myself. *Ouch, that hurt. Better take things steady for a while.*

The nurse checked me over, then attached a plastic cone to my collar, wrapping it tightly around my head. I couldn't see the ground and I stumbled as I struggled to walk forward. The nurse held me as I got my bearings. I couldn't turn my head to the side without banging myself with the cone. The room spun as I looked around. I sat down.

"Come on, it's time to go home. You don't have to stay here."

I padded to the door. As soon as we walked into the main area, I could sense Alyson was on the other side of a small door in the corner. I skidded over to it, pulling the nurse behind me, the plastic cone crashing into the door. *Hurry up, hurry up, let me out.*

I squeezed through the opening door, squashing the cone against the wall in my haste to see my mom again. *There she is.* My heart was pounding in my chest, blood surging through my veins. I felt light-headed and giddy as I raced over, whirling around, trying to get close to her as she wrapped me in her arms. I wanted to nuzzle her and lick her, but the cone was in the way, so I settled for a deep whine and a sigh as she hugged me.

"Oh, my baby girl. I've missed you so much." She whispered calm words to me, stroking and holding me, and dropping soft kisses onto the end of my nose. "You're going to be alright, and we can go home now."

The nurse smiled at us. "She sure is glad to see you again."

"You've no idea how much I missed her today." Alyson thanked the nurse, attached my lead, and we walked outside. I was desperate for a wee, but as I leant over towards a wall and lifted my leg up, the cone crashed into the brickwork, sending me sprawling. I crouched down instead, and the relief was instant. *How am I supposed to get used to this? I hope it's not permanent. I can't possibly go to sleep with this thing wrapped round my neck.*

We walked over to our car, and I stopped and waited for Alyson to open the door, jumping up onto the back seat as usual. *Ouch, ouch, that hurt.* A razor-sharp pain tore across my back, like a hot knife slicing through my skin.

"Oh no, Kat, you're not supposed to jump anywhere yet. I was about to lift you up. Are your stitches okay?" Alyson leant into the car, her face inches from mine, her eyes wide. Her hand fluttered as she stroked me and I settled down on the seat. The pain subsided, and I licked her hand.

She drove home, then lifted me off the back seat, popping me onto the ground. *That's better.* We went for a quick walk. I kept bumping into the parked cars with the front edge of the cone, but I managed to go for another wee without falling over. Walking up the drive to the front door of our house, I stopped for a second. I had never been more pleased to see that door opening and Dave standing inside.

An enormous bowl of roasted chicken and a new dog food awaited me. It was softer, and I wolfed it down. I licked my lips. My mouth was still numb, and my head was foggy, as if someone had stuffed it full of newspaper.

"She's had two teeth extracted and her teeth cleaned as well as removing the lump," Alyson said to Dave as I settled on my bed in the kitchen. The blasted cone got in the way as I attempted to rest my head on my paws. I shuffled round, trying to get comfortable.

"The nurse said to leave the plaster on for twenty-four hours, then soak it off gently. The stitches will apparently dissolve in a few days. We have to take her back next Sunday to be checked over, but they said the surgery went really well."

"When will we get the results?" Dave asked.

"They promised to ring me as soon as they know. They've sent the tumour off to Lisbon to be analysed. It was larger than they thought it would be. They had to cut out quite a lot, so the operation was more complicated than expected. She's not allowed to walk very far for the next ten days, and no jumping. Although no-one told Kat, and she leapt straight up into the back of the car. I felt awful, but she seems fine."

"What about the cone? Does she have to wear that? It looks so uncomfortable."

"I don't know. They just said not to let her touch the wound. But I can't imagine she'd be able to reach the top of her back, anyway. She's always with us, so we can watch her. Let's take it off and see how she fares."

Alyson reached over and unhooked my collar and untied the plastic cone. I shook my head, glad to be rid of the cumbersome thing, and settled down again. It had been a long day, and I was tired.

Soaking the plaster off the next day proved to be harder than it sounded, as it was stuck firmly to my skin. I tried to be brave, but I yelped as Alyson peeled it off my back. I turned around, trying to see what had happened to me. The skin was taut and out of shape, as if fastened in place by an invisible wire. It rippled when I moved. After a few days, the pressure eased, and I could walk more freely. I tried not to lie on my back, though.

The first time I caught it on something, I squealed. A low-lying branch of a tree got in my way as I shimmied underneath to sniff something interesting. I had forgotten my back for a second, and the pain shot through my brain as the branch scraped across the wound. I was far more cautious about where I sniffed and crawled after that.

Then the important day arrived. Alyson received a call from the vet's and she grabbed her phone. Dave huddled in behind her, trying to listen in at the same time. She flapped her hand at him as she moved away; the nurse was talking in a fast, excited tone to her. As usual, I could only hear one side of the conversation.

"Oh my goodness, are you sure?"

"So, can you repeat that, just so I'm clear? Yes, your English is very good. And in Portuguese then. *Benigno.* Benign."

She put her thumb up to Dave and grinned; her smile reaching right across her face.

"The tumour was benign. And you got it all. The scans are clear. Thank you so much."

Alyson sank into a chair. Dave reached over the sofa and gave me a big hug. I snuggled into him and looked over at Alyson. She had tears rolling down her face as she sat hugging her knees.

"You're alright Kat. You're going to be fine." She came over and hugged Dave, with me squashed underneath. They were one gigantic mass of arms and bodies, both holding me and laughing and crying. I wriggled out, it was hard to breathe underneath all that, and sat watching them, my tail wagging. I didn't understand everything, but I knew they were happy, and I was okay.

But why they were crying was still a mystery to me. I decided humans were a strange bunch sometimes. But as I looked over and saw the love in their eyes for me and felt Alyson's kisses on the top of my head, I knew everything was going to be alright.

CHAPTER THIRTY-TWO

The wound from the surgery soon healed and Alyson told me I had an impressive eight-centimetre scar etched across my lower back. They had shaved me down to the skin, which made it look even more severe, but as my fur grew back, the scar became almost invisible. I knew it was there, though, and if I spun around and twisted my body too quickly, a sharp pain would shoot through me.

Life soon returned to its normal pace, although Dave and Alyson were constantly busy. If they went out, they took me with them whenever they could. I was always happy to tag along and meet new people and find fresh places to sniff and explore.

"D'you remember the artist, Jan, and her husband? We met them at that lunch the other week?" Alyson was in the office sat in front of her computer.

"Yes, he was called Chris, I think. I liked them," Dave spluttered, his mouth full of toast. "Why?"

"She has some paintings I quite like. I wouldn't mind seeing them in person. She's invited us up to their house in the Alentejo. There's a map here."

Dave leant over her shoulder and peered at the screen. "That's about an hour away. It looks like a scenic route via Monchique. Yeah, let's go for it."

Alyson called her and arranged to meet them. The next day, we all jumped in the car and Dave tucked me onto the back seat, wrapping a blanket around me and placing a cushion beside my head.

"It's quite a long drive, Kat, so settle down and have a snooze."

I rested my head on the cushion and closed my eyes. I kept waking up, but the car was still moving. The journey seemed to last forever before Dave finally pulled into a long driveway and I sat up and yawned.

We were in the countryside. I jumped out of the car. There were fields and trees in the distance surrounding a well-tended garden with a pretty house nestled in the centre. A dog bounded up to me, wagging his tail. He seemed friendly, and I followed him over to a flowerbed for a wee. He sniffed me cautiously, and I returned the compliment. Introductions over, I wandered off to explore, almost bumping into a friendly faced lady.

"Hello Kat, I'm Jan." A man behind her opened the front door of the house. "And that's Chris." He patted me on the head and greeted Dave and Alyson. Everyone seemed happy to see each other as we all trooped inside the house, and I followed the dog into the hallway.

"This is Bert," Jan said, as the dog trotted past me into the kitchen. He sauntered over to a metal bowl lying on the floor and stood eating something. The aroma of rich, meaty dog food and biscuits wafted in my direction. *Turkey, if I'm not mistaken.* Saliva pooled in my mouth and dribbled onto the floor. I knew I had to be polite and wait, as it was Bert's house, not mine. But oh, the food smelt good. *I hope he leaves some for me.*

Bert licked his lips, slurped some water out of a plastic bowl beside the food, then sauntered off and sat licking his bum. *Charming.*

I scampered over, eager to see if he had left anything behind. *Result.* The bowl was still half full. I dived in, scoffing the lot in a few quick seconds. It tasted divine, all the better for being Bert's food and not mine. I sat back on my haunches, savouring the last morsel stuck to my chops, then froze.

"Oh no, Kat, what have you done?" Alyson came rushing over to me. "Oh, I'm so sorry. I think she's eaten Bert's food."

Chris was standing nearby. He chuckled. "That's alright. Don't worry. Serves Bert right for not finishing his lunch. He never eats his food quickly. We usually put a bowl down for him in the morning and he comes and goes when he feels like eating a bit."

My ears shot upwards. *He doesn't eat all the food they give him? How can he possibly leave that delicious meat and crunchy biscuit lying in the bowl?* I shook my head. *Utterly ridiculous. He's obviously never had to live on the streets and fend for himself, eating any scraps he can find on the floor or in the bins.* Bert didn't even seem particularly bothered that I had eaten his lunch. It was most odd.

We became friends after that day, and we often visited their home as Alyson and Dave got on well with Jan and Chris. They came to see us too, and Bert was one of the few dogs that I welcomed into our house. I drew the line at him sleeping on my bed, but he was good company and a perfect gentleman. Sadly, they never left his bowl of food on the floor again. I always trotted straight into their kitchen, though, every time we visited their house, just in case…

I had been living with Alyson and Dave for about four years. It was hard to count the length of time exactly, but I was happy and settled. One morning, all that changed when I overheard them chatting.

"I think it's time to sell up, don't you? We have so much space here we don't use, and we've still got the mortgage going out each month. We could buy something smaller and not have any debt."

Alyson nodded. "Yes, I agree. We've been here long enough. Time to move on to somewhere new."

Something plummeted inside me. I couldn't understand everything they were saying, but I knew the word move. I didn't like it. *What if they move and leave me behind? Or give me away to someone else? What if there isn't room for me anymore?*

They didn't reassure me like they normally did if they were talking about something important. I stored the conversation away in the back of my mind. It was like a goblin sitting hunched inside me, taunting me. I replayed their words in my head so many times they haunted me.

Over the next few months, lots of strange things happened. Different people kept visiting our house and wandering through all the rooms. Some of them were nice to me and fussed over me, but others ignored me completely. I didn't like those folks very much.

One couple kept coming round and measuring things, pacing around the rooms and talking amongst themselves. Alyson didn't seem bothered and left them to it, which I thought was extremely odd.

Then things became even more strange. Boxes appeared in all the rooms and Dave and Alyson were always busy. Things kept disappearing around me. I went out for a long walk with Alyson one afternoon and when we returned, the furniture from one of the bedrooms was missing. More and more boxes arrived, and Alyson kept stuffing things inside them. I hid my toys, but she found them anyway and put them into a big box, sealing the lid with tape.

"Here you go, you can keep tiger and your rabbit. I know they're your favourites," she said as she picked up the box with my toys in and moved it to her studio.

I followed her, keeping a close eye on where that box ended up. After sniffing it, I reassured myself that I could tell which one it was later if I needed to. I was worried. All of Alyson's painting gear had gone. The floor was bare. I sniffed the air. It felt different now. As if someone had pulled the heart out of our home and left the bare walls behind.

I had nightmares that night for the first time in ages. I dreamt I was alone in a forest. A winding, sinister path stretched ahead of me, and an owl was screeching, his cry echoing across the sky. The trees loomed over me, dark branches reaching out, gnarled fingers of timber stretching over my head. The leaves whistled as the wind picked up strength, blowing against me and forcing me down into a heap on the ground. As I lay shivering in the cold, the branches of the trees creaked and groaned. I was completely alone.

I ran through the trees, looking for Alyson and Dave. The wind was shrieking as I reached the end of the forest and looked out over a precipice. My legs only just stopped in time, my claws scrabbling to gain a hold in the soil. I was on the edge of a cliff. I peered down. The dark, whirling sea whisked up like soup boiling in a cauldron, the waves bubbling and crashing far below. I could feel myself falling. There was no one to save me. I woke whimpering and shaking.

"What's up baby? Did you have a bad dream? It's okay, I'm here." Alyson curled up with her arm around me and fell asleep again, but I was awake for ages. *You're here now. But what if you leave me? What if you move away and don't take me with you?*

I spent the next few days on high alert. I couldn't settle at all. And then our waterbed disappeared. The bed I had spent every night sleeping in beside Alyson. Gone. I walked round the bedroom, sniffing the space where it had been. Another empty room. I didn't like what was happening.

We moved into the spare bedroom downstairs, but it wasn't the same. I tried to get comfortable, but slept fitfully. Alyson kept tossing and turning in her sleep, as I lay there watching her.

The next day was crazy. We went for our normal walk, but Alyson didn't let me stop and sniff everything like she usually did. As soon as we returned home, she dashed around, throwing things into boxes, and answered the doorbell as a giant van pulled up onto the driveway. Three men bounded into the house and started picking things up and taking them out to the van.

I retreated to the lounge and sat on a chair, trying to keep out of the way. After a while, everything went quiet, and I panicked. I couldn't hear anyone. *Have they all gone and left me behind?*

I raced downstairs and skidded out of the studio door, then sighed with relief. They were all sitting in the garden. Alyson was chatting with one of the men, who pointed over towards me and said, "Oh, do we need to pack your dog up and load her in the van too?"

I stopped dead; my feet frozen on the spot. I tried to move my paws, but they were like concrete blocks, cemented in place.

"No, silly. As if I'd do that to our girl." Alyson laughed and walked over to me, patting me on the head.

"Come on, Missy, let's pack up the last of your toys and get things ready for tomorrow."

So that's it, is it? Tomorrow is the big day. Is tomorrow the day you leave me? I trudged inside behind her as she packed even more things into boxes. I went to sit on my bed in the kitchen, but she picked it up and stuffed it into a bin bag.

"Sorry, Kat, this one needs to go in the van. But I've kept a bed for you in the spare room. Don't worry."

Don't worry? That's easy for you to say. My entire world is turning upside down in front of my eyes. And all my things are being packed away.

The next morning, the men returned and started filling up another van with boxes. We walked out to our car, and I jumped onto the back seat. Dave and Alyson loaded up the boot and clambered into their seats.

"Say goodbye to our old house," Alyson said, as the car gathered speed.

That's it then. I saw our house fading into the distance and wondered where we were going.

We drove over the bridge to Portimão and parked up outside a café. *Is this it? Are we only going this far?* I was confused.

We walked over to a table. Mark, one of their friends, was sitting there. We joined him and they sat chatting, then Alyson and Dave got up to leave. I stood up too.

"No, you stay here with Mark. I won't be long." Alyson handed him my lead, picked up a folder and set off down the road.

I've never stayed with Mark before. Have they gone and left me here with him? I know she said she'd wouldn't be long, but... Alyson looked so distracted and Dave walked off without even glancing back at me.

They entered a building nearby, and the door slammed shut behind them. Mark picked up his things and stood up. "Come on, let's go for a walk."

We wandered around the harbour, then back to the café, and I stared at the building they had disappeared into. *Maybe if I keep watch long enough...*

Finally, the door opened, and Alyson and Dave came back outside. I shot up, wagging my tail as they returned to the café, and Alyson gave me a big hug.

"We did it, girl. We sold our house and bought another one." Alyson was jigging around. "We're off to live in Aljezur. You're going to love it there."

My head was spinning. *Did she just say we're going to live somewhere else? Together?* They were taking me with them. The tremendous weight I had been carrying soared off my back and flew away, like an eagle taking to the sky. *It's okay. We're all going to stay together. We're off to somewhere new.*

I realised how silly I had been. *Of course they love me. Alyson has promised me she would always be my mommy, and that we'd always be together.* I perked up. Their enthusiasm was infectious.

I didn't know where Aljezur was, but as long as I was there with Alyson and Dave, it didn't matter. Home was wherever they were.

CHAPTER THIRTY-THREE

Alyson and Dave were in high spirits as they drove along, and I stared out of the window trying to see where we were going. We turned onto the motorway, and I settled down. I knew that meant we were in for a long drive. Then the road changed to winding lanes bordered by trees and fields. I perked up.

We drove through a small town and parked up on a quiet street. I jumped out, eager to see our new home. I could smell cows and goats. And chickens. Alyson and Dave walked up to a house on the corner and opened the front door. I wriggled past them and trotted inside.

"Euw! Even without the old musty furniture, it still smells bad in here." Alyson wrinkled her nose. "But it's all ours. And it will be fab once we've sorted it out." She whirled around, rubbing her hands together, and grinned at Dave.

"Yes, it's a fantastic house. But I'm glad we booked those cleaners for today. What time are they coming?" Dave dropped a load of bags in the hallway and walked back out to the car. More bags and boxes came in, along with my fluffy bed. It amazed me how much they had managed to stuff into the boot of the car.

"Four o'clock. So we have plenty of time. It's only just midday. It's amazing how quickly we got everything done and signed at the notary. We were only homeless for thirty minutes!"

"I know. It all went so smoothly." Dave dumped another box in the lounge. It seemed huge and so empty. Their voices echoed around the room, tumbling across the tiled floors and bouncing back off the empty walls.

"I held my breath as the lady went through our paperwork, though. I can't believe I was stupid enough to leave that box lying around without labelling it. Everything we needed at the notary was in that box. The removal man said it was one of the first things he loaded into the van. Thank goodness our solicitor had a copy of everything. And I had our passports in my bag. I shudder to think what would have happened if I'd put those in the box too." Alyson's face dropped.

"Well, we wouldn't be standing here with the keys to our new home, that's for sure. But we are, so everything worked out fine in the end. Let's have a look around. See if it's as we remember it."

"Yes, it's been ages since we viewed it. I can't believe we got it for the price we did. It's incredible how everything turned out. After losing that other house when we had put the offer in, I was starting to panic. I didn't think we'd find anything. And then you found this place. You clever thing. And it's perfect." Alyson reached over and kissed Dave.

"I know. It literally ticked every box on our list. It was meant to be." Dave walked into the kitchen, and I followed him. There was a stale odour in the air. Like someone had cooked lots of fried food in there with all the doors and windows shut.

I trotted round, trying to get my bearings in the empty rooms. The big room was obviously the lounge, with patio doors opening out onto the front garden. And it had a proper fireplace in the corner. That was exciting. Alyson and Dave had friends with a fireplace in their lounge. I loved it when we visited them in the winter, and I could curl up on the floor in front of the flames.

There was another room that looked like a bedroom, but it was downstairs. Then a small bathroom. I wasn't going in there; it had a shower in it. The kitchen led into another room with an even bigger sink. One door led to the garden and another to the garage. The garden was strange. There was nothing there. Just a few paving slabs and a pile of earth. It looped around and out to where Dave had parked our car on the driveway.

I went back inside. There was more to explore. Over to the front door and up the stairs. *Ah, that's more like it.* Two large rooms, they would be our bedrooms. Dave prowled around, opening wardrobe doors, and looking inside. Another bathroom too. I peered around the door. It was enormous. It had a bath in it with a shower over the top. Another no-go area for me. *You're not getting me in there in a hurry.*

Another door off the landing led to an outside terrace and balcony. The walls had patterned bricks with holes in, and they were the perfect height for me. I stuffed my nose through a gap and looked out onto the street. I could smell chickens again. *I need to find out where they are.*

I trotted downstairs and almost bumped into Alyson, who was skipping around. "I love it. We're going to be so happy here."

Dave picked up his keys. "Come on, I'm starving. Let's go into town and grab some lunch. There's that little café by the bridge. They do nice food."

We jumped in the car and drove back along the main road, parking up in a gravel car park. I leapt out. *Hang on a minute, I recognise this place. We've been here before. There's a walk along the river from this car park. I like it here.* I sniffed around me. Yes, it was definitely the same town.

"Let's take Missy for a quick stroll before lunch. She must be bursting by now." Alyson gathered up her things and hugged Dave. "I'm so excited we're here."

I scampered off, sniffing and exploring. The path was soft underfoot, lined with plants and bushes, with the river on one side and open fields stretching far away into the distance on the other side. It smelt wonderful, earthy, and fresh. A brilliant blue sky stretched overhead, like a shining dome cradling the earth. Trees bordered the path, their branches arching overhead, leaves tinkling and twirling in the gentle breeze.

We walked a little way, then Alyson stopped and called me back to her. "Time for lunch, little one. But we'll explore all of this later. You see far over there in the distance? That's where our new house is. We can walk out of the front door and down the road and we'll join this path at the other end. This will be our walk each morning. All the way round to the road and back home. We can enjoy a river walk every day. Aren't we lucky?"

I couldn't believe it. *Is this really where we're going to live?* It was so much nicer than our old house, which had been on a main road, surrounded by concrete and other houses. This was open countryside, with fields and paths and the river. And lots and lots of fantastic smells.

We strolled back into town and crossed a tiny bridge over the river. I stopped, my tail wagging. There were ducks on the water, paddling and bobbing around, heads held high. I was desperate to go down there and play with them, but Alyson said no. *Maybe later.*

We sat at a café, and I slurped some water and scoffed a biscuit. I stretched out, basking in the sunshine as Dave and Alyson had lunch.

"What time did you say the cleaners were coming again?" Dave asked, twirling his spoon around his coffee cup.

"Four o'clock."

"Well, it's half three, so we'd better make a move."

"No way! How can it possibly be that time already?" Alyson shot up out of her chair, almost knocking the table over. I jumped up with a start, shaking myself. I *might* have nodded off for a while. It was so nice and warm sat there.

We hurried back to the car and drove home. It was such a great feeling, looking up at the new house and knowing we were going to live there.

Alyson took me for a walk up the road while Dave busied himself unloading more things from the boot and carrying them inside. There were four little streets, and an interesting lane that stretched away up the hill. A dog bounded out of a garden and came up to say hello. He was a bit goofy, with black fluffy fur and a dopey expression, but he was friendly. I presumed he lived in one of the houses, but as time went by, I realised he spent all his time outside.

A property at the top of the road enticed me over. They had a plot of land with an array of tumbledown sheds, and scrabbling around outside were lots of chickens and ducks. I scampered over for a closer look and took a deep breath. *So this is where the chickens are.* They smelt amazing. I stood by the fence watching them rummaging in the earth with their claws, as one stood up and stretched out its wings, beating them in the air and squawking loudly.

We ambled down the road. I could tell how happy Alyson was as she bent down to pat me on the head. She was grinning from ear to ear, and her eyes were glowing. "We're going to love it here, Missy. Look at that view. We're surrounded by fields and farmland, and we can walk beside the river every day." She hugged me. "Come on, let's go back and see the cleaners and make sure they're okay."

The house was a flurry of noise and people dashing around.

"They seem to know what they're doing," Dave said as we walked into the lounge. "Let's leave them to it and go for an early dinner. We can't do anything to help and we'll only be in the way. I told them we'd be back at eight thirty."

"I'll just grab some food for Kat, then. Give me a minute." Alyson dived into one of the bags and picked up some things. Then we trooped outside and walked down the road.

"Our favourite pizza place. Right at the end of the road. Perfect." Dave rubbed his hands together and winked at Alyson.

We settled outside at a table, and I ate all my dinner up, then sat with a hopeful expression on my face as the waiter brought out two enormous plates. Giant pizzas. They were so big they were hanging off the sides of the tray, strings of gooey cheese dripping down. They smelt divine. *I wonder if I'll get any?* They never gave me food from the table; I knew that. But I could always dream.

The plates were sadly soon shining and empty, as the waiter returned carrying two bowls of chocolate mousse. It wasn't fair; the food smelt so good. I looked up a few minutes later and all I could see were two gleaming glass bowls on the table.

"Sorry, Missy. Not for you." Alyson actually had the audacity to lick her lips as she spoke to me.

I sighed. They paid the bill, and we walked back to the house.

"I hope they've finished cleaning. We need to get the beds set up and get sorted out." Dave opened the door to be met by a flustered lady waving a cleaning cloth in the air.

"It was even worse than you said it would be. We'll be at least another hour. Sorry."

"That's alright, don't worry. Have you done upstairs?" Dave looked at her and motioned with his hand for her to slow down.

"Yes, all finished up there. I'm sorry it has taken us so long. It really was filthy."

"I know. I'm sorry. We thought it might be. The last owners didn't look after the house very well."

"Well, it's a lovely place. But I'd better keep going else we'll be here until midnight." The lady went back into the kitchen.

Dave picked up a large bag and groaned. "Gosh, that's heavy. Right, I'll start getting the airbeds sorted so we can sleep tonight. Everything else will have to wait until the morning."

"I'll find the bedding." Alyson went upstairs behind Dave, and I followed as he placed a bundle of rubber on the floor. He pressed a button, and I shot backwards. It was alive.

"It's okay, Kat, it's just air going into the mattress. Nothing to worry about."

The thing expanded to an enormous size, almost filling the room. I walked over and sniffed it tentatively. Alyson climbed onto it and lay down and I put a paw out and touched it, then scrabbled up beside her. The bed wobbled beneath me, and I ended up sprawled out, crashing my back legs into Alyson's side.

"Well, this will be fun. When do the new waterbeds arrive?" Alyson laughed and ruffled my head.

"Not for several weeks, unfortunately. So you pair had better get used to your new bed." Dave joined in the laughter.

Alyson rolled off onto the floor and started giggling, as I tried to stand up but felt my legs sink underneath me. I collapsed back down, then stood up slowly, my feet wobbling. I jumped off and skidded across the floor.

"Yep, this is going to be hilarious." Alyson put a sheet on the top of the mattress and dug out our pillows from a bag. "It'll have to do until the beds arrive."

We waited for the cleaners to finish, then Alyson took me out for a last stroll up the road for a wee, before we headed up to bed. The mattress still felt weird, but I was so tired I curled up beside Alyson and fell straight asleep, dreaming about our new home, the funny bed, and our furry feathered neighbours.

CHAPTER THIRTY-FOUR

The next morning, I woke up, turned over, and almost rolled off the bed. As Alyson yawned and stretched beside me, I carefully placed my front paws on the ground, then slipped off the inflatable mattress, ending up in a heap on the floor.

"I hope our new beds arrive soon, Kat. I don't fancy sleeping on this once it gets colder." Alyson shook herself and got dressed as I wandered round, sniffing the corners of the room. It still smelt funny, stale odours now mingling with a flowery bleach scent.

We set off on our walk, going straight towards the river at the end of the road. I scampered ahead to a small metal bridge and peeked through a gap in the railings.

"Hopefully, there will be lots of water there in the winter." Alyson pointed, and I looked down with interest. Water meant animals and ducks. "Although it's certainly bone dry at the moment."

We walked along a dusty path that meandered beside the river on our left. Fields stretched out on our right-hand side all the way to the main road in the distance, but here on the path, it was calm and peaceful. Birds were twittering and singing in the trees that lined the walk, and a blackbird skipped along in front of us.

We sauntered through a section of bamboo that arched over the path. It was like walking through a green iridescent tunnel, the arms of the plants snaking upwards and almost touching each other above our heads. The path widened as more trees came into view, their leaves rustling and whispering as we passed them. An enormous white bird, wings tipped with black, flew overhead. The whoosh of its wings startled me as it swooped past us and Alyson looked up, delight etched across her face.

"A white stork. Fabulous. Look, over there, it has a nest perched on that old water mill. I love being surrounded by nature. It's gorgeous here, isn't it?"

I trotted along, sniffing everything in my path. The scents were terrific, there were so many animal smells and plants to savour. There was a little stream of water trickling along the riverbed as we neared the town. As the water hit the rocks below the surface, it gurgled and tinkled a tune of its own and then, suddenly, I saw it. A duck paddling along, head up, beak pointed to the sky. Alyson was right. Nature was all around us. It was amazing.

The path led to the car park we had stopped in the day before. We crossed the road and Alyson walked over to a small café and ordered a coffee. I sat beside her, watching as she chatted with the owner, and I wolfed down a biscuit and some water.

After Alyson had finished her coffee, we explored the other side of the old town. The river here was teeming with ducks, twirling around, pecking at each other, and waddling along the embankment. My tail quivered with excitement.

Alyson gasped and pointed at the water. "An otter." Her voice was soft, almost reverent, as she leant over the railings to get a better view. I couldn't see anything except a swirl of water, but Alyson seemed delighted with whatever was below the surface. Suddenly, a tiny nose and two beady eyes peeped up out of the water. Alyson let out a long sigh. "Perfect."

We walked back along the road and arrived home. My legs were quite tired, and I was glad to scoff my breakfast then lie down for a snooze.

That became our daily routine, walking the river path and

stopping for a coffee at the café. Alyson loved getting up with the dawn and being out just as the world was waking up, and I eagerly followed her. The air was always fresh and the sky clear and bright so early in the morning, and our walks filled me with a spark of energy that fizzed through my veins.

The first few days in the new house were strange, but then the removal men arrived with our things and it felt like home once Alyson and Dave had unpacked everything. They had a brand-new sofa delivered, which was enormous. A huge L-shaped set of chairs that locked together, with space for me to stretch out and sleep. I picked the spot nearest to the fireplace, of course, and eagerly awaited the day it was cold enough to light the fire.

Our new waterbeds finally arrived. I hid in the lounge and waited for them to be built. I remembered the fun Dave had getting our old waterbed emptied when we moved, so I kept out of the way. That night, curling up asleep beside Alyson on our new bed, was heavenly.

Slowly, Alyson and Dave spruced things up. Painters came and decorated inside and out, and a builder sorted out the garden, putting up a big roof and creating a covered area. Another sofa arrived and Dave manoeuvred it into place under the roofed section outside, next to a dining table and chairs. That meant I could sit on the sofa and watch while they ate lunch every day in the garden, which was a splendid arrangement from my point of view as I could see what they were eating.

The third room downstairs became an office, and I had a soft cushioned bed tucked under Alyson's desk. They turned the second kitchen into Alyson's art studio, with another bed placed on the floor for me beside her easel. Dave joked I had more beds than the Queen, as he positioned another fluffy bed in the kitchen, squashed in alongside the table.

I loved the fact I had a space in every room that was mine. Alyson understood my need to feel safe and to know where my place was. I enjoyed being beside her all the time. I didn't mind what she was doing as long as I could keep her company. And sleep came easier to me if she was nearby. She promised she'd watch over me when I was asleep, and I believed her.

If she had to go out somewhere without me, Alyson always kissed my nose and whispered the same words in my ear: "I'll miss you, and I'll be back as quickly as I can. I'll always come back, don't worry. I love you." I would watch as she drove away, keeping a lookout sitting on the sofa near the patio doors.

I might fall asleep, but always with half an ear up listening, waiting for her car to return. My instincts were never wrong. I could sense when Alyson was on her way. She would hug me and kiss me as soon as she walked in the door, laughing as I whirled around in excitement. Everything was alright once she was back home.

I grew to love Aljezur and especially the little neighbourhood we lived in. There were only a few houses and lots of the people had a dog living with them. I didn't mind saying hello to them, but that was about it.

One dog that became more than an acquaintance, though, was the goofy black ball of fur we met on our first day. Alyson found out his name was Valente, and he became an almost permanent fixture on our morning walks. He turned up at the gate one morning as we were about to leave for our walk and joined us. After that, he would sit outside our house waiting for us most mornings. I didn't mind too much. He was very polite to me, and he didn't get in the way.

Alyson began carrying some food for him, too. He spent all day in the road and was obviously hungry most of the time. I think he slept outside at night in the summer months, and he was quite lonely. So when we stopped, and she gave me my biscuit and water each day, she would tip some food on the ground for Valente too. He always wolfed it down so quickly I felt sorry for him.

He had a funny walk that made Alyson laugh. She said he had four paws that moved in four different directions when he ran, but he was always happy to be out with us. He didn't come with us though if it was raining, which I found very amusing.

One morning by the river we had quite a shock. The rain clouds were gathering, so obviously there was no sign of Valente. The sound of squealing reached my ears as we walked along, but I didn't know what it was. As we got closer, Alyson stopped and grabbed my lead from her pocket.

"Come here Kat. Let me put your lead on. I don't want you to go near that."

I trotted ahead a few steps and looked down at the riverbed. There was no water there, just dry soil, and I couldn't see what she was talking about for a second. Then I spotted it, on the far side of the bank. A small black or dark brown pig. It was hard to tell the colour exactly, as it was half-hidden in the bushes. But its squeal was unmistakable. The herd had left it behind. And it wasn't happy.

"I'm not too concerned about that little fella," Alyson said as she hooked me up and held me close to her. She looked around and behind us, frowning. "But what I am worried about is his mom or dad hearing the squeals and coming back to find him. I don't fancy meeting an angry *javali*, thank you very much." She sidled past the section of the river and I followed her. The squealing finally faded into the distance as Alyson breathed a sigh of relief.

I didn't know what a *javali* was, but Alyson later told Dave about our encounter.

"Ooh, you don't want to get too close to one of those. They can be really nasty creatures." Dave spun round in his chair and his eyes widened.

"That's what I was worried about. The last thing I wanted to see was an irate mother crashing through the bushes, thinking we were attacking one of her litter."

Alyson looked them up on the internet. "Yes, see here. Wild boar. I knew they were around the area. You can hear the local farmers hunting them on a Sunday morning. The guns going off drive Valente mad. He shoots off home the minute he hears the first crack whistling in the distance. But I've never actually seen a *javali* before."

She pointed to the screen. "Blimey, look at this. It says here that the average adult male weighs seventy to ninety kilogrammes. Females are smaller, forty to sixty-five kilogrammes." She gasped. "But occasionally both sexes can reach up to a hundred-and-fifty kilogrammes in weight. And they have an incredible sense of smell and hearing. They can capture sounds imperceptible to man, allowing them to detect food and enemies over one hundred metres away and even discover food buried in the ground."

"That's why so much of the soil along the riverbank is dug up some mornings, then. They like to eat roots and plants. Look at the teeth on that one," Dave said, leaning over Alyson and staring at the screen. "Crikey. Good job one of those didn't come after you this morning."

"Yeah, thanks for that. You know how to make a girl feel better, don't you?" Alyson laughed as I settled down on my bed.

Think we'll give that one a wide berth then, if we spot it again.

CHAPTER THIRTY-FIVE

Fields and animals surrounded our house. One of our neighbours had chickens and ducks, and the house at the top of the lane was like a farmyard. They had chickens, geese, ducks, four goats, three pigs, two dogs and a donkey. Alyson said it was a Christmas carol, and we were only missing the partridge in the pear tree. There were plenty of orange trees instead, though.

My favourite was the house with the rabbits. Sometimes the owner, Luis, let me in through his garden gate. I would scamper past the rows of birds in cages, all chirruping and tweeting, and head straight for the wooden huts made out of old crates at the rear of their yard.

I could smell them long before I reached them. A crisp fresh aroma of hay mingled with corn and something else sweet and musty. Their little noses twitched as I approached, their back legs kicking the wooden floor as they tried to move away. I tried to stick my nose inside the crate to get a better sniff of them, my tail wagging as I panted and looked to Alyson for help. *If they could just open the lid and lift me inside...*

One summer, another house nearby had a litter of rabbits. Ten pure white babies, fluffy and adorable. The neighbour, Fernanda, housed them in a small shed on a piece of unused land round the corner from us. We walked past them every evening. I loved to sit in front of the fence and watch them hopping round, wiping their faces with their little paws. They seemed to stare around in wonderment at the world. They quickly grew to their full adult size, although Alyson said they would soon be 'for the pot'. I didn't know what that meant.

One night, Alyson took me out for my quick last walk up the road for a wee before bedtime. We walked out of our gate and I stopped in amazement. There, in front of me, was a rabbit, standing in the middle of the road, nose twitching. Another hopped out from the grass verge to join it, then another.

I was so excited I couldn't wait and rushed headlong forward, startling the first rabbit, who shot up in the air. His back legs thrust upwards as he leapt up the road. More rabbits came bounding out of the grass and they soon surrounded me. I couldn't decide which one to chase first. I didn't want to hurt them. I just wanted to play with them, but they were not happy and raced away, scattering in all directions.

"Come on you. You're frightening them. They must have found a way out of their shed. Now, do we tell Fernanda?" Alyson hugged me, then whispered in my ear. "I don't think we'll tell her, eh? They can have some fun at night for a while, instead of being locked up in that little shed."

For the next few nights, we saw them prancing and bouncing around the road, and lolloping through the abandoned garden of an old house that no-one lived in. I was in heaven, watching them as they stood up on their hind legs, their noses quivering as they saw me. I learnt to sit still and not disturb them, but one night it was just too much for me as I leapt forward to get closer to them. They scattered in a flurry of fluffy tails, scampering away from me, their back legs thumping the ground in protest.

Eventually, Alyson told me Fernanda had found a hole in the shed which she fixed by reinforcing the wall, and the rabbits' night-time capers ended.

I grew to like the goats that lived at the top of the lane too, and

Alyson adored them. They were owned by a delightfully crazy man called Felix, who seemed to be permanently happy. Alyson would stop and chat to him. He told her he worked at the cemetery, digging graves, and that he loved to stand looking over the valley and tending his animals. He said it was his way of making sense of life and death.

One day Alyson asked him about the goats.

"What are their names?"

"They don't have names," Felix replied, lifting up his hat and tipping his head to one side. "Why do they need a name?"

"I think they should. See that one over there? She loves eating branches from the olive tree. You should call her Oliveira."

"Okay," he said, laughing. I think he was warming to the idea. "What about this boy here?"

"He strides around. He's funny, with his little beard and stocky legs." Alyson stroked the goat's head behind his ears and he stared up at her with a cute expression on his face.

"He likes you." Felix scratched his chin and replaced his hat on his head at a jaunty angle. "He reminds me of our famous footballer, Eusébio."

"Then that's what we'll call him." Alyson pointed to another girl, a lovely brown goat with piebald white patches on her back. "And she should be Margarida."

"That just leaves one more, then." Felix pointed to a tiny goat, half the size of the others. She had wary eyes and held her head low.

"She's just a baby, isn't she? How old is she?" Alyson fondled her as I tried and failed to get behind the goat to sniff her bum. She wasn't having any of that, and jumped away from me.

Felix guffawed. "No, she's almost three years old. She's a miniature goat."

"Oh, wow. I thought she was the baby. Well, how about we call her Nina then? Like *menina*, little girl, but shorter?"

"That'll do." Felix pointed at his donkey, who was busy chomping on the grass in the field beside us. "I'm guessing you're going to give him a name, too?"

"Oh, I've already named him Dave. After my husband."

Felix roared and slapped his thigh. "That's funny. He should have a Portuguese name, too. Jeremias. I'll call him Jeremias."

The donkey snickered and shook his head.

"See? He approves." Felix clapped his hands.

"Well, I'm still going to call him Dave."

Later Alyson told Dave about the grand naming ceremony that had taken place. He chuckled when he found out the donkey's name.

"But why are you bothering to get him to name his animals?" Dave asked her.

"It's important. He'll look after them better now they have names. You'll see. He's made a connection with them now."

Alyson was right. From that day onwards, Felix was more affectionate towards his animals, and he even cut the rope that tethered the donkey's front two legs together, letting him walk freely. The goats were still attached to ropes when they were in the fields, but Felix looked after them well and fed them each day. I saw Alyson smile to herself when she heard him calling Nina by name one afternoon, as he patted the goat's head.

One set of creatures less welcome were the ticks that lived in the fields and seemed to like me rather too much. Alyson bought a special collar for me and wound it around my neck. I didn't like it at all. It smelt horrible and made my skin prickle. The collar was supposed to stop the ticks from making themselves too comfortable and setting up home in my fur, but it didn't always work.

One night, we returned from our night-time walk; it had been a particularly exciting time as I had spotted a hedgehog snuffling through the long grass. I have a love-hate relationship with them. I want to sniff them, but I never let myself get too close. This one spotted me, rolled up and fanned out his spikes. I knew better than to put my nose near those.

I scoffed my bedtime biscuit, then raced upstairs and jumped on the bed. Something crawled across my skin, burrowing through my fur. I was busy sniffing and licking my back legs when Alyson walked into the bedroom.

"What's up with you, Missy? What are you scratching at?"

She lifted my leg and shot backwards.

"Urgh! What's that? Oh no, it's a tick!" She adjusted the cover on the bed. "And another one. And another. There are loads of them crawling around."

I must have disturbed a nest on our walk. Alyson leapt around, waving her arms in the air, and reached across to her bedside table. She snatched up a roll of masking tape and started ripping off lengths of it, dabbing them on the bedcover. Each time she picked up a tick, she folded the paper over on itself, trapping it inside. *That's clever.* I made myself comfy on the bed, enjoying the show.

"Oh, there are too many, Kat. I've counted twenty-seven already. And there are more crawling out of you. They're so tiny. You must have the entire nest of them on you."

She threw the roll of tape onto the bed.

"There's nothing else for it. Come on you, bath time." She picked me up, making the 'oof' sound she always made when she lifted me up. Apparently, I was quite heavy. She marched into the bathroom and dumped me in the bath, calling to Dave to come and help.

How could she do this to me? I hated having a shower at the best of times, but this was bedtime. I bent my head and waited for the blast of warm water to hit me, as Alyson lathered up a disgusting-smelling shampoo. Suds flew everywhere, and the liquid seeped into my eyes. *Ouch, that stings.*

I shook myself, sending shampoo flying up the wall and all over Alyson and Dave. *That'll teach them, dragging me in here at night.* I tried to sulk afterwards, but Alyson tucked me up so nicely in bed that I forgave her.

I didn't understand how dangerous the ticks could be until one afternoon Alyson came downstairs and walked over to Dave.

"Look at this bite on my leg. I think it must have been a tick. It's really sore." She showed him a red patch on her thigh, and he looked at it and frowned.

"Better keep an eye on that. It looks nasty. The tick isn't still in there, is it?"

"No, I don't think so," Alyson replied, peering at her leg. "But I don't feel too great. I'm going to lie down for a while."

I followed her upstairs and lay on the bed beside her. I didn't like the look of her. She was hot and sweaty. I knew something was wrong, as I curled up close to her and licked her hand. She fondled my head, groaned, and fell asleep.

CHAPTER THIRTY-SIX

I woke up and looked over at Alyson. She was lying in bed beside me, still asleep. Her face was shiny, with beads of sweat pooling around her eyes and temple, and she was moaning quietly. I wrinkled my nose. There was a strange odour in the room, like fruit that had gone bad, or stale, mouldy bread.

She stirred and rolled over to face me. "Hello, you. I don't feel too great, Missy."

Dave's face dropped as he came into the bedroom. His brows puckered together, and he made a low clucking noise.

"You don't look too good."

"I know. I feel awful. My head's pounding, my neck's sore, and I'm a bit dizzy." Alyson tried to stir, but her head sank back onto her pillow.

"Don't get up. Stay there. Can I get you anything?"

"Just a glass of water, thanks." Alyson closed her eyes.

Dave returned with the water and sat on the side of the bed, touching Alyson's arm.

"Try to get some sleep, love. I'll take Kat out this evening for you. Hopefully, you'll feel better in the morning."

I could see the concern etched in his eyes as he stood up. "Come on, girl, time for your walk. You'll have to put up with me tonight."

I jumped off the bed, glancing back at Alyson.

"It's okay. She'll still be here when we get back. We won't be long."

We went up the road together. I did my business as quickly as I could, wanting to return home to be with Alyson. I didn't like how she looked at all.

That night, I settled down on the bed beside her and lay watching her for ages as she tossed and turned in her sleep. The funny stale odour was coming from her pores. I could smell it more clearly now, and it wasn't pleasant.

The next morning, Alyson was worse. Sweat covered her face and dropped onto her pillow, and her hands shook and fluttered in her sleep. She groaned as she woke up and heaved herself up to a sitting position. It was a few moments before she even saw me lying beside her. She reached out her hand and touched me.

"I guess that tick bite is making me ill. But don't worry, Kat, I'm a fighter. I'll get through this." Her face softened and tears formed a haze over her eyes as she talked. "But I don't think I'll be taking you out for a walk for the next few days, little one. We'll have to trust Daddy to do that. I love our walks so much. But I'll be fit again soon and we'll be back having our adventures."

Dave came in, rubbing his hands over his eyes. "Gosh, I don't know how you guys get up so early every morning." He yawned, his mouth opening wide, as I hopped off the bed. "Come on, Kat, let's go for a walk. You'll be okay here while I'm gone?" He stroked Alyson's cheek.

"Yes. I'll be fine. You guys have a good walk."

It was strange going out without Alyson. I trotted along as Dave wandered beside me, but he didn't chat to me the same as Alyson did. It seemed wrong being out there in the beautiful spring sunshine, with the birds chirruping in the trees, the air fresh and crisp. *I shouldn't be enjoying this without my mom.* I snuffled around for a while, then turned to head home.

"Is that it? Don't you want to walk any farther?" Dave stopped and twirled my lead in his hands.

I carried on walking home, and he followed me. "You want to get back to make sure your mom is okay, don't you? She'll be alright, don't worry."

I scoffed my breakfast and raced upstairs to settle on the bed beside her. She was sleeping, and I tried not to wake her as I lay down, resting my head on my paws. Her breath sounded wheezy, almost rasping, as she took short, sharp gulps of air.

Dave came in and she stirred. "Any better, love?"

"No, not really. I think I've got a temperature. My skin is all claggy and horrible."

"A temperature? How high?" Dave peered down at her; his eyes shining.

"No idea. But I feel hot."

"I'm going to the chemist's to buy a thermometer."

"You don't need to do that." Alyson shook her head.

"No, I do. It'll be fun finding out how hot you are."

"Oh, very funny. Bugger off."

Dave chuckled. "I'll be back soon to take your temperature."

He picked up his car keys, and the door slammed shut.

I fell asleep, waking with a start as the front door opened, and Dave bounded up the stairs. He ripped open a packet and brandished a thermometer with a flourish.

"Ta-da! Now we can find out how bad your fever is."

Alyson perched herself up on her elbows, and Dave placed the thermometer in her mouth.

"Just be grateful you're not a cow... or a dog." He looked at me with a gleam in his eye and I winced as I remembered the last time I had visited the vet's. *That's not funny, pal. You try having something like that stuck up your bum.* He removed the plastic vial and squinted at it.

His eyes widened as he opened his mouth to speak, then closed it again. He stared at the thermometer.

"Oh, that's not good."

"What? What's not good? Tell me. What does it read?"

Dave showed her. "One hundred and two." He shook his head. "I'm no expert. But that sounds high. I'll look it up on the internet. Back in a mo."

He went downstairs, returning a short while later.

"It's... erm, not great. If you hit one hundred and three, I'm supposed to call an ambulance."

"Don't be daft. There's no need for an ambulance. I'll be fine. I just need to sleep it off." Alyson turned over in bed and huffed.

"Well, I'll come back in a few hours and test you again. I'll bring you up another drink, but you need to eat something, too."

"I'm not hungry now. Maybe later." Alyson closed her eyes.

"Keep an eye on her for me, Missy." Dave ruffled my fur and adjusted the blind at the window, tipping it down further to stop the light from flooding into the room.

"Mmm, that's better. No bright light." Alyson was already half-asleep, murmuring to herself. I settled in beside her and fell into an uneasy sleep. Each time she moaned, I woke up. I had a bad feeling about it all. *She shouldn't be ill like this.*

🐾 🐾 🐾 🐾 🐾

"One hundred and two point four." Dave shook the thermometer and his eyes narrowed. Alyson stretched out, her face contorted with pain. It was later that evening and I sat motionless, watching them talk.

"Right, I'm calling an ambulance."

"No, you're not. You said one hundred and three. I'm not there." Alyson grabbed hold of him, her fingers gripping his arm. "No ambulance. Do you hear? I'm going to be fine. Give me another night here. I'll be alright tomorrow."

"Well, if you're not, and your temperature is still that high, I'm ringing then. No arguments."

"Okay." Alyson curled up, wrapping an arm around her head.

Dave beckoned me to go for a walk, and I left her side slowly, reluctant to leave her.

"She'll be fine for a few minutes, Kat. Come on, you need to go out."

I raced back home and settled down beside her, trying to lick her hand to reassure her and make her better. I'm not sure she realised I was there as she tossed around, the duvet almost on the ground, as her arms flailed in the air.

The next morning, I woke just as the first light of dawn crept through the window. It was eerily silent in the room. Alyson was breathing more quietly, and the awful stale aroma had disappeared. I snuffled my nose in her hand, wriggling in closer to her. She murmured and stirred slightly. I lay beside her, licking her gently, willing her to be alright. I couldn't even begin to imagine life without her. She was more than just my mommy; she was my soul mate. My everything. My constant companion, my alpha.

Dave came in and Alyson opened her eyes. The corners of her mouth lifted and her eyes seemed a bit brighter.

"How are you feeling, my love?" Dave caressed her cheek and wiped his hand over her forehead.

"A little better, I think."

"Let's test you again then and see." He held out the thermometer, and she placed it under her tongue, her eyes rolling as she grimaced. "Nergh uh."

"You can't talk with that in your mouth, silly. Hang on a sec." Dave laughed as he took the thermometer away and angled it towards the light from the window.

"Well, what's the verdict?"

"Ninety-nine point seven."

"Yay, that's more like it."

"Yes, it is. But you're not out of the woods yet, young lady. And you must eat something."

"I could manage a bowl of porridge, I think. Just a small bowl."

"Okay, coming right up after I've taken Missy out for a quick walk."

The day passed quietly. Alyson ate some porridge and later

devoured a bowl of mashed sweet potato Dave cooked for her. "You must be feeling a bit better," he said, as he picked up the empty bowl.

"Yes, a little. I'm still woozy. And my head is throbbing. But I'm not so hot or clammy anymore."

"If you are up to it tomorrow, I think we need to get you to the health centre to see a doctor." Dave handed her a fresh glass of water and sat perched on the edge of the bed.

"Let's see how I am. But that sounds like a good idea. I'll need some medicine to fight this. I'm assuming it must be the tick bite that caused this. I've heard tick fever can be nasty, but I'd no idea how bad it could be."

"Well, get some rest now. We'll see how you are in the morning."

Dave switched off the light. "I'm guessing you're staying here, Missy?" He patted my head. "Kat hasn't left your side, has she? She's such an amazing girl. She knows you're ill, bless her."

I was almost offended by that statement. *My mommy is ill. Of course I'm not leaving her.* I settled down, snorting my disgust for all to hear.

Alyson dragged herself out of bed the following morning and I listened to the water running in the sink in the bathroom. She returned with her face washed and sat on the bed. Dave took me out for a quick walk and when I returned, she had got dressed and was downstairs in the kitchen.

"I think I'll manage that trip to the health centre now. Let's go before I run out of steam."

They left me on the sofa and drove away. I positioned myself on the seat nearest the window and waited until I saw them return. Alyson wobbled a little as she walked, as Dave held her arm and guided her through the front door.

She bent down to hug me, then groaned as she straightened up. "I'm going back to bed now," she said and trudged up the stairs.

"I'll sort out this medicine and bring you up your first tablets."

Alyson's mouth twisted as she lifted her eyes upwards, chin jutting out. "Okay."

She climbed into bed as Dave entered the bedroom, carrying a glass of water and two packets. "Right, you take one of these in the morning, for eight days. And you have two of these every day, one morning, one evening, for seven days. I've written it all down on the packets so we don't get confused." He popped out two tablets from their blister packs and handed them to Alyson.

She pushed them around her palm with her thumb. "Look at the size of these tablets. Are you sure they're for me and not a horse? They're huge." She tutted and grabbed one, swallowing it with a gulp of water. Her body shuddered, and she shook her head.

"Yuck. That was horrible." She repeated the exercise again, then leaned back against the headboard. "Well, the next few days are going to be fun."

She sank down under the duvet, and I curled up beside her.

CHAPTER THIRTY-SEVEN

That evening Alyson woke with a jolt, leaning forward in bed and almost knocking into me. I wondered what had made her move so quickly.

"Can you see them? Over there?" She pointed to the wardrobes lining the far wall of the bedroom.

What is she talking about?

"Those hazy figures over there. They look like they're made of smoke. Like wisps of light, shimmering and swirling."

She's definitely lost it. I looked over to where she was pointing. *Nothing. How could there be anything or anyone in the room without me knowing? Preposterous.*

She wiped her arm over her face, then smoothed the duvet with her fingertips. "I keep seeing things, Kat. And having awful dreams too."

I nuzzled up to her, snuffling my nose into her hand, and tried to reassure her everything was going to be alright, but inside I was worried. *What's going on? Why is she seeing things?*

She fell back asleep. It was the middle of the night when she screamed out.

"Nargh! Nooo. Help!"

I spun round, shaking the sleep from my head. *What's wrong?*

Alyson was shaking, her hands gripping the duvet around her body. Her eyes narrowed, her gaze darting round the room.

"They were here again. And this time, a figure dressed in a shiny metal suit was beside them. Like the Tin Man from the *Wizard of Oz*, except this man had a chainsaw in his hand. Blood was dripping from the metal teeth. And he had this manic face, shining purple, eyes bulging. It was horrible."

I had no idea what she was talking about, but I could see how upset she was. I crawled over and licked her hand and arm.

"Oh Kat. I think I'm going mad. I'm too scared to go back to sleep, in case they return. And I can feel my heart racing and pounding in my chest. It sounds so loud, like a drumbeat. Bang, bang."

It seemed an eternity before a bright orange sunrise lit up the sky. Alyson was still muttering in her sleep. It had taken ages for her to settle again. I had kept watch, willing her to stop shaking, and I yawned as Dave came into the room.

"Morning Missy. How's our patient today?"

Alyson stirred and looked up, her eyes blinking in the light. "I've had the most awful nightmares. And I keep seeing things in the room. They seem so real."

"That must be horrible. This tick fever is a nasty thing, isn't it? But I can't believe it's causing you nightmares. That doesn't sound right."

"I don't want to go back to sleep. I think I'll try to get up this morning." Alyson dragged herself up to a sitting position, then wobbled slightly. "I feel giddy."

"Well, you can stay right where you are, then. You're not getting up. I'll take Kat out, then come back and check up on you. Stay there."

Alyson didn't argue with him. That wasn't a good sign.

I went out for my walk with Dave, scoffed my breakfast, then rushed upstairs. Alyson was sitting holding a book, her eyes glazed.

"Good book?" Dave said as he entered the room.

"No. I can't concentrate at all. I keep reading the same paragraph over and over."

"Well, I've discovered something that might put your mind at rest. I checked online. Those tablets the doctor prescribed for the tick fever. They usually give them to people with typhoid. The side effects are pretty horrendous. And they include nightmares and hallucinations."

"That explains it, at least. I thought I was going mad last night. I've never had such vivid, scary dreams before. And when I woke up, it was as if the characters in the dream had floated out of my head and were in the room here with me. I couldn't tell if I was awake or still asleep. Poor Kat, I must have frightened her. I was so scared." She patted the bed beside her, and I jumped up and snuggled my head in under the crook of her arm.

"There, you'll be okay now. Missy will look after you. Try to rest. And here, take the next lot of tablets."

Alyson grimaced as Dave handed her the medicine. "Great. Just what I need. More nightmares."

She downed them swiftly, swigging back a glass of water. "Yeuk! They're revolting."

"Sorry, love. But you must take the entire course of treatment. The doctor was adamant about that."

"I know. I'll be alright. We'll get through this, won't we, Kat?"

"Course you will. But next time, leave the ticks behind when you go for a walk, eh?"

"Ha, yes. Like I wanted a tick to attack me. I didn't even realise I had one on me until I noticed the bite on my leg. That's the trouble. They're small enough to hide. All you need to do is walk through the wrong bit of grass and they jump onto you. It probably crawled in over my sock and up my leg."

"Yes, that's almost certainly what happened. That new collar we bought seems to work well for Kat. She hasn't had any more ticks since we placed it on her." Dave patted my head and fingered the tick and flea collar attached to me.

"Hey, that's an idea!" He pointed to the collar and then over to Alyson. "Maybe we can get one in your size to wrap around your neck, too?"

"You know what you can do with your daft ideas, don't you?" A low chuckle escaped from Alyson.

"Oh, you're feeling a bit better, then? Try to rest, love, and don't worry. I'm sure you'll be alright again soon."

"I hope so. I miss walking Kat so much. I hate lying here like this."

"Just hang in there and let the medicine do its thing. You'll be up and about in no time."

🐾 🐾 🐾 🐾 🐾

In reality, it took a further two weeks before Alyson was well enough to take me out for our morning walk. Every day, I saw her looking through the window, watching as Dave set off down the road with me, her face etched with sadness.

Finally, the day came when she sat up in bed with a determined expression. "Come on, Kat. Let's do it."

She got dressed, her hands shaking slightly. "Gah, I need to get a grip." She walked downstairs, grabbed my lead and called to me. "Time for a walk."

It was a beautiful morning. The sky was a haze of pale peach and purple breaking through the early mist that lay like a soft shawl draped across the distant trees. I stopped, sniffing the air, and looked over at Alyson. She was standing still, her arms stretched out wide, her head slightly back, face tilted up towards the sky. Her smile lit up her eyes, and her cheeks were glowing. She took a deep breath and exhaled slowly.

"Ahh, that's better. I feel alive again. Come on, little one. Let's go explore."

My alpha was back. All was well with the world. I scampered after her as she marched off towards the river. Never had a morning walk felt so good.

In the days that followed, Alyson slowly regained her strength. Listening to her conversations with friends about her experience was highly amusing. If she was talking to an English expat friend, it went something like this:

"I had tick fever, but I'm okay now."

"Oh, poor you. I bet it wasn't very nice."

And that was it. But if she mentioned it to a Portuguese friend, the conversation progressed very differently:

"I had tick fever. I was quite ill."

"Tick fever? Oh, no!" A startled expression and wild waving of arms in the air frequently accompanied this loud exclamation.

"Tick fever is very dangerous. I know someone that had tick fever."

There was usually a pause at this point, obviously inserted for dramatic effect. The person's eyes would widen as they leaned in closer to Alyson and whispered, "They died."

CHAPTER THIRTY-EIGHT

One of my favourite people in Aljezur was a local Portuguese lady called Maria Victoria. The first time I met her, I knew she was special, as I trotted over to say hello. She reached down to pet me with such affection in her eyes, as Alyson stopped to talk to her.

She lived near us on the road up to the main square in Igreja Nova, in the new part of town. Her daughter and family lived at the end of our little street, and it wasn't long before Maria Victoria became a close friend.

Alyson told me she trusted me completely. If we met someone and I liked them and let them fuss over me, Alyson knew they were okay. But if I pulled away, or worse, hid behind her, that was my warning that all wasn't well. It happened a few times. A man came to repair the toilet in our house and fit a new shower screen, and I took an instant dislike to him. I tried to growl a warning, but Dave let him in the house anyway, and he made a mess of all the work he did. Much to Alyson's annoyance, he even fitted the shower screen upside down.

But Maria Victoria was special. She was a sprightly, plucky character who marched everywhere. You could spot her in the distance, wearing a fisherman's hat perched jauntily on her head. She was often wielding a wooden walking stick and always carried a shopping bag that was usually stuffed full of grasses and plants she had plucked from down by the river. She lived in a small, traditional house with a plot of land beside it that became one of our regular places to visit.

We walked up to her house one afternoon and Alyson chatted to her as I moseyed around, sniffing and checking every corner of her little outside covered seating area. Maria Victoria had a cat, a fluffy ginger thing who always taunted me. I suddenly spotted him perched on a wall, looking down at me. I tried barking at him a few times, but he had an imperious expression on his face that said, 'Go on then, make me move'. He even closed his eyes as I barked, which infuriated me. *Doesn't he know he's supposed to be frightened and skulk away?*

I got my own back one day, though. Maria Victoria had left her back door open and while she was busy gossiping with Alyson, I sneaked through the hanging bead curtain and snuck into the kitchen. On the floor, tucked under the table, was the cat's food bowl. It was full of delicious, fresh, meaty food. Well, it *was* full of food, until I scoffed it all.

I trotted back outside but made the fatal mistake of licking my lips as I sauntered past the cat.

"Oh no, what have you been up to? What have you been eating?"
Blast! I forgot Alyson had a sixth sense about me and my mischief.

I tried to look nonchalant, but I peered down and saw a piece of meat still stuck to my nose. Alyson was staring at me, her head comically slanted to one side. I licked up the chunk of meat, but it was too late. She had spotted it.

"I'm so sorry. I think Kat has eaten the cat's food." Alyson giggled. It did sound funny when she put it like that.

"No problem," said Maria Victoria. "I've plenty more." She pointed at her garden. "You'll want to go over there and have a look. I've got new baby chickens."

My ears pricked up. *Chickens? Let's go.* I scampered off down the path that ran alongside her house and up to my special place, Alyson following behind me. At the end of her plot outside, there was a set of stone steps that led up to the roof of the house next door. I could sit on those steps and look down into Maria Victoria's garden, right beside the old sheds that housed her chickens. They had an outside run with a slope inside leading up to the fence beside the steps. It was the ideal layout for me.

I stuck my nose to the metal fence and sniffed. There it was, that unmistakable aroma. Corn and grass and slimy poo. *Chickens.* I could see them, all fluff and feathers, scrabbling around and squawking as they bumped into each other. They were busy eating the cornmeal scattered on the ground, pecking at each other and squabbling over the scraps.

That became my treat for the next few weeks, going up to see the chickens. Maria Victoria gave Alyson a handful of lettuce leaves one day, expecting her to throw them over the fence, but Alyson sat with the lettuce in her hand, patiently calling to the chicken she had named Eric. He was the smallest and scrawniest of the bunch, always getting picked on by the others, but slowly Alyson gained his trust. Eventually he would spot us arriving and run up the slope when she called him, ready to eat the lettuce leaves from her hand.

It was the perfect setup for me, as I perched on the steps and stared into their enclosure. I could almost put my nose through the gaps in the fencing panel, as Eric placed his head alongside the fence, one beady black eye glinting at me. I had to be careful, though. One day he missed the lettuce leaf Alyson held out for him and almost jabbed my nose.

We walked up there one afternoon and I climbed up my steps and sat down, then looked over at the fence in dismay. Maria Victoria had fastened a sheet of plastic mesh across the fence, and I couldn't see into the pen. She walked over and Alyson pointed out my sad face to her, as she stood there holding a wilting piece of lettuce.

"Oh, Maria Victoria, why have you put the net there? I can't feed Eric anymore, and Kat can't see her friends."

Maria Victoria chuckled. "You and those chickens. They're for the pot soon, you know. The boys anyway. I'll keep the girls. They'll go in with the main brood, as they'll lay eggs for me."

"Oh no, you can't do that. Not little Eric." Alyson's face dropped as I listened to them talking.

"Yes. Sorry. That's life."

It sounded more like death to me.

The next afternoon, I trotted up the steps and sat waiting for Alyson to catch me up. She walked over to the fence, then stopped and pointed.

"Look at that." She laughed, then reached forward, removing a peg attached to the mesh. Someone had cut a slit all the way up the material, which Alyson pulled back and clipped up out of the way.

Hurray! I could look into the pen again. Eric immediately scurried up the slope towards us, bickering loudly and squawking. He was obviously hungry. I settled down to watch.

"I hope you like my solution," a voice said. Alyson and I both jumped. We were so busy with Eric, we hadn't heard Maria Victoria approach us.

"It's perfect. Thank you so much," Alyson said, as she pushed the last pieces of lettuce through the fence.

"Well, make the most of it. They'll be gone by the weekend."

Sure enough, the next week we went back, and it was quiet as we approached the end of the garden. Too quiet. I clambered up the steps and peeped inside. Nothing. It was empty. Eric had gone. And so had all his friends.

Maria Victoria popped her head around the corner. "Don't worry. Eric is safe. He's in the freezer. I'm saving him for Easter." Her laugh echoed around us. "But I'm going to the market next week to buy some baby rabbits."

Did she say rabbits? I perked up.

The rabbits duly arrived, and they were fabulous. They smelt even more enticing than the chickens, as I settled down in my favourite spot to watch them as they scampered around. Alyson tried to train them the same as Eric to hop up the slope to be fed, but they were too dopey for that. They were so comical, lolloping around, all floppy ears and fluffy tails. They would stamp the ground, then stand up on their back legs as they ruffled their little faces with their front paws.

"They're for the pot too," Maria Victoria said as she ambled up to us.

"Oh no, not the rabbits as well." Alyson's face fell as she stared through the fence.

"Yes, they'll all go the same way as the chickens." Maria ran her finger across her throat and cackled. "Although rabbits are different." Her arm reached up again, and she placed her hand behind her head. Her fingers ran around the back of her neck.

"Chickens, front of the neck. Rabbits, back." She walked off, still laughing to herself.

"Those poor rabbits, Kat. We need to do something."

That night, Alyson sat typing away on her computer, then ran a piece of paper through the printer. She went out to her studio, and I followed her as she set up a machine. Soon the paper whirred through it and came out glossy and shiny.

"There. I'll put that on the fence tomorrow. We'll try to save the bunnies." She picked up the piece of paper and punched holes in it, just as Dave walked into the room.

"What have you got there?"

"It's a petition. To save Maria Victoria's rabbits from being slaughtered. I'm going to pin it to their fence tomorrow. Just for a bit of fun."

The next day Alyson took the shiny paper and attached it to the fence with zip ties. Maria Victoria came over and didn't see it at first, then she roared with laughter.

"*Salve os Coelhos—Petição*" ("Save the Rabbits—Petition"), she read aloud. "You've even signed it. And added a paw print for Kat beside your signatures, and three photos of the rabbits. Well, I never."

I could hear her chuckling as she walked all the way back to her house.

Sadly, the petition didn't work. A few weeks later, we wandered past Maria Victoria's garden. She was hard at work leaning over something. A knife gleamed in the sunshine, as Alyson suddenly stepped backwards and screamed.

"Is that what I think it is?" she asked, as Maria Victoria stepped aside, revealing a rabbit hanging upside down from a tree branch. Its skin was peeled away in one long strip, blood dripping from its head as one eye gleamed menacingly at us. Alyson turned her back on the scene.

"I can't bear to look," she said, as Maria Victoria laughed.

"It's just life. That's what we do round here. The rabbit will make a lovely dinner for my family. And then I'll buy some more. Raised and fed with no chemicals. Just good, plain, healthy food."

I was glad that Maria Victoria didn't have any plans to eat me. We walked home, and I waited for my dinner to be prepared.

"Chicken and turkey braised in gravy with roasted vegetables," Alyson said, looking at the label on the tin of dog food as she set my bowl down on the floor. "I think they do a rabbit flavour as well."

I looked up at her. Sometimes I wished I could talk so I could tell her what I was thinking, although at that moment, it was probably best I said nothing. The chicken and turkey in gravy tasted delicious, though.

CHAPTER THIRTY-NINE

Sadly, Jeremias' freedom was short-lived. The donkey had become increasingly restless, and Alyson had grown wary of getting too close to him. She still took him a carrot when we walked up the lane, but held it at arm's length, waiting for him to walk to the end of his rope before feeding him. He had even grazed her arm one afternoon in a half-hearted attempt to bite her. I kept my distance from him. He was far too big for me.

We went out for a lunchtime stroll up the road, and I was busy snuffling around and didn't realise what had happened at first. We reached Felix's house, and Alyson stopped in the middle of the road and gasped aloud.

"Oh my god, no, what's he doing?"

I looked over and saw Jeremias in the field opposite us. He was prancing around, shaking his head, and snickering. He must have freed himself from the rope that was tethered to the ground and had escaped into the field that Felix had left the goats grazing in. I could only see two goats there, Nina and Eusébio.

Suddenly, Jeremias lunged over and snatched Nina up in his mouth, tossing her into the air. I couldn't see where she landed. Two men, workmen from a nearby house, rushed outside and ran over to the field. Jeremias careered over and grabbed Nina again, throwing her up over his head. Alyson called to me. I raced over to her, and she bent down and gathered me in her arms.

"Oh no. Not Nina. She's pregnant," she called out to the men. One of them ran behind the donkey, trying to reach Nina, whilst the other waved his arms and shouted, trying to shoo Jeremias away. Alyson's face was white. She looked terrified as she dropped me to the ground and pushed me against a small electrical box beside the road.

"He's gone mad. Look at him galloping around the field. What if he comes after us?" She tucked me in beside her, pushing her legs against me. "I'll protect you, don't worry."

I could hear my heart pounding as I watched Jeremias hurtling across the field. One man came over to us, his face etched with pain. "She's in a bad way. I don't think she'll make it. She looks like she's dying."

"The goat? No, please don't say that. She's pregnant." Alyson's voice was a mere whisper as she hung her head.

Jeremias lurched over to Eusébio and hefted him into the air, hurling him to the ground. My heart seemed to stop beating as I peered around the side of Alyson's leg. The donkey was looking straight at us. He scratched the ground with his hoof, and gave his loud, braying cry.

"Oh god! No. He knows us. What if he comes this way? You're the same size as little Nina. He could easily pick you up too, Kat." She pushed me further down onto the ground with her leg, as the donkey careered round the edge of the field towards the road where we were standing.

Just before Jeremias reached us, the other man jumped in front of us, waving his arms and smacking the donkey. Jeremias skidded away across the road. He spotted the ducks in their enclosure and trotted over to look at them, turning his back on us.

"Quick Kat, now's our chance." The open road stretched before us. Apart from a couple of parked cars, there was no protection at all for us. Only the road, and a deranged, mad donkey, who could certainly move faster than we could.

Alyson told the men she would try to call the owner, Felix, and get some help, as she reached down to touch my head. "Come on, girl, we'll have to make a run for it. Stay close to me."

She didn't need to tell me that. My paws were shaking as we crept past the ducks. Jeremias was staring at them, presumably wondering how he could jump over the fence to reach them. I broke into a run, Alyson keeping pace beside me, until we reached the end of the road and our house.

Alyson sank to her knees, hugging me. "Oh Kat, that was awful. Poor Nina. I can't believe Jeremias would attack the goats like that." Her voice trembled and her hand was shaking as she grabbed her phone from her pocket and started making phone calls.

"Blast. Nobody's answering. Felix must be busy at work."

I could see Jeremias was still lurking around near the ducks. I hid behind Alyson, wondering what was going to happen. A neighbour came up the road, walking his dog.

Alyson gabbled at him in Portuguese, explaining what had happened, and he promised to ring round and get some help. We went inside our house and Alyson called Dave, who was at a photo shoot. As soon as she heard his voice, she started crying.

"It was horrible. Jeremias was loose. There were two men. He picked up Nina and tossed her into the air. She's pregnant. He said she looked like she was dying."

"Slow down, hang on a minute." I could hear Dave's voice on the speakerphone. "You're not making any sense. Who threw Nina in the air? One of the men?"

"No, not the men. Jeremias. The donkey. He picked her up and tossed her up over his head. Twice. Then he picked Eusébio up and threw him up in the air. It was awful. He's still up there now, prancing around."

"That bloody donkey. Well, at least you and Kat are safe."

"I kept thinking Kat's the same size as Nina. And Jeremias knows us. He came straight at us. One of the workmen got in the way, thank goodness. Then we raced down the road. I didn't know I could run that fast."

ALYSON SHELDRAKE

"I can't believe a donkey would do that. He's obviously gone mad, poor thing. Stuck up there all day on his own. I'll be home soon. I'm already on my way. Stay there. And don't do anything heroic. Stay home with Kat."

"Oh, don't worry. I'm not going back up there."

Alyson called me over onto the sofa and lay holding me and kissing the top of my head. "Kat, that was so horrible, wasn't it? And poor Nina. What if she doesn't make it?" I felt her tears dripping onto me as she buried her face in my fur.

Dave came home and gave Alyson a big hug and sat chatting to her.

"It was so awful, watching that crazy donkey. He just grabbed Nina like she was a rag doll, flinging her into the air. And she's due soon. Her first ever pregnancy. I chatted to Felix about her. It was Eusébio, of course. He's the father. We joked about how proud he looked, strutting round the field. And now this has happened."

They had lunch as Alyson checked her phone.

"It's Felix. He's sent me a message. She's alright. Little Nina. And he can still feel a fluttering inside her belly. Eusébio is fine, too."

A few days later Alyson said she would risk us going back up the road again. Felix told her he had hobbled Jeremias' legs together and got a new stronger rope. He had tied him up in another field further away until he could find a new home for him.

I walked up warily, looking around me in case Jeremias was nearby, but he was nowhere to be seen. Ahead of us was a commotion. Felix and his neighbours were all huddled up in the road, staring down at something. As we got closer, Alyson gasped. "It's Nina. She's given birth."

I hurried to keep up with her as she raced up the road. She wouldn't let me get too close, but I peered through her legs as she held me beside her. Curled up in the grass by the side of the road was a tiny weeny baby kid goat. Nina stood nearby, munching on the grass, now and then stopping to nudge the little one. The baby bleated, a small, pitiful sound as she squirmed around. Blood was dripping from Nina's rear.

"She's a girl. She's fine. Nina was great. I hardly had to do anything to help her." Felix stood nearby, his arms folded, a great big smile on his face. One neighbour was cooing and aahing over the baby. Alyson was captivated, her face beaming as she bent down to look at the little furry bundle.

The neighbours left as Alyson stood chatting to Felix.

"Well, are we going to name her Margarida, then? In memory," he asked, grinning at her.

"Yes, that's what we agreed, if it was a girl."

I knew that the older goat, Margarida, had died. I remembered an afternoon when she was lying sick in the shelter area, nestled on a bed of straw. Alyson had knelt down, stroking her and whispering soft words. She wiped away a tear as we left, saying to me, "She won't be here tomorrow, Kat. She's too ill to survive."

And now there was a new baby goat. A new Margarida. I tried to move closer. I was longing to snuffle her and smell everything, but Alyson wouldn't let me. She called Dave on her phone and he came up the road to join us. Felix went back to work as Alyson stood watching.

"She's not moving very much. Don't you think she should be feeding by now?"

Dave looked over at the kid. "I'm not sure. Felix seemed to think she was alright. But she looks lethargic to me. I don't know much about goats. Nina doesn't appear too interested in her."

"I'm going to fetch some food for Nina. She loves the leaves of the cork oak tree at the top of the road. I'll be back in a minute."

Alyson returned clutching a handful of branches and climbed up onto the bank, where the little bundle was now lying motionless. She called Nina over and I wondered what she was going to do.

Oh, that's clever. Alyson had placed the branches close to the baby, so that when Nina wandered over to eat them, she would be near to her little one.

"Come on, Margarida. You need to eat. Come and find your

mommy." Alyson stroked her and the baby opened her eyes and snuffled around. She stumbled to her feet, her legs wobbling and unsteady as she swayed. She took a faltering step forward, then sank back down, her eyes blinking.

"Come on, that's it. Good girl. Try again."

Nina was busy munching on the leaves as Alyson gently nudged her sideways.

"Look at this enormous mark on her back where Jeremias the donkey bit her," she said to Dave.

"I still can't believe she survived that attack. And now, here she is, with her little girl delivered safe and sound. It's a miracle."

Alyson positioned Nina directly over her baby as the kid lifted her head up, her mouth opening and closing as she struggled to feed.

"That's it. Here they are." Alyson tried to point Nina's udder towards the baby. Margarida suddenly reached up and grasped a teat, sucking, then fell back to the ground, bleating. She tried again, more successfully, as Alyson let out a quiet cheer.

"There you go. She's feeding now."

I sniffed around. The scent of the birth was everywhere, and my nose was itching. I was so desperate to smell everything. I wrinkled my face up as I snuffled the grass. Then, all too soon, it was time to go home. I turned my head to look at the tiny baby goat. She was on her feet, grasping at Nina's belly, as we walked away.

CHAPTER FORTY

I was getting older. Sometimes the joints in my legs swelled up. I couldn't walk as far, and I slept more during the day. One morning, I hobbled home from our walk. The pain was like someone had shot a hot rod through my back legs, and I stumbled and almost fell twice.

Alyson looked at me and I could see the love pouring out of her eyes like a river of pure light. "Don't worry, little one. We'll grow old together. I will always love you, forever. You have nothing to fear."

She went to the vet's and returned with some tablets, which she sneaked into my breakfast each day. I knew they were there and swallowed them reluctantly. After a few days, though, I could move easier, and the pain disappeared. Unless it was a damp, wintry morning, when my legs were like solid planks of wood. I would wait while Alyson massaged them for me, her hands deftly soothing the soreness and stiffness away. She seemed to know the days I needed a little extra help.

Alyson's love for me was incredible. It was almost a physical thing, like a warm, soft blanket cushioned around me. I never believed I was special before I met her, but she made me feel as if I was the only dog on earth that had ever been loved this much. She watched over me, stroked and groomed me, fed me, walked me, spent every day with me, and slept beside me. I basked in the affection and care she showered over me.

In return, she was my alpha, my everything. I wished I could tell her how much I loved her too, but I think she knew. It was as if there was an invisible thread that tied our hearts together. I only had to glance at her sometimes to know what she was thinking and to experience a fresh surge of love bursting through me.

Her gentleness and compassion were all-encompassing for me, and she had a sixth sense for when I needed help. I was convinced she could read my thoughts. If I needed to go out for a walk, I just nudged her gently with my nose against her leg. She'd look at me and understand what I was asking. If I had a burr stuck in my paw, she would stop walking and reach down to remove it for me. In return, I would lick her hand in gratitude.

"You're such a darling girl. You're saying thank you, aren't you?"

She knew.

I fell asleep every night beside her, knowing I was warm, safe, and loved, with a belly full of food. It's all any dog ever wants in life. And I had it in abundance. Her last words to me each night were, "I love you. Night, night. Sweet dreams and see you in the morning."

I would snuffle my reply and settle down with my head resting on my pillow. I was utterly content and loved beyond my wildest imagination.

Never once when I was cold and alone in that barn, or later wandering the streets in Spain, did I imagine I could feel this way. Or that we would end up helping another dog to have the same wonderful chance of a life filled with love.

One afternoon, we were walking home from Maria Victoria's house. She had a new batch of chickens and it had been a fun afternoon watching them scurrying around, all feet and feathers. As we strolled along the road, I looked over towards the river. The local people had divided the field into parcels of land, each plot cultivated and tended lovingly. Crops of vegetables shone in the late afternoon sun, lines of cabbage plants and beans stretching neatly into the distance.

A flash of yellow darted beside one of the storage areas. Alyson must have seen it too, as she stopped and shaded her eyes with her hand. The sun was low in the sky and shining directly at us. By the time we reached the spot, a young dog raced away across the field. The dog was obviously frightened and alone. There was no-one else around. It ran off, and I thought I wouldn't see it again, and started to walk on. I then noticed the dog had doubled-back and was standing still, looking over at us.

Alyson whistled, and the dog took a few tentative steps forward. It kept creeping towards us, hesitating, and hiding from view, then reappearing each time Alyson called it.

Finally, the dog was within about ten metres of us, still hiding in the long grass and crouching down. It was extremely nervous and wary, although obviously interested in us. Alyson called again, and the dog bounded out of the grass and landed in front of me. She was a girl, a young pup, no more than a year old, and she was shaking all over.

Alyson always carries a small bag of my kibble food in her pocket, and she scattered some on the ground. The pup gobbled it up, not even stopping to check around or gauge her own safety first.

She bounced up to me, spun round several times, then sat and stared at me. She was a pretty dog, despite the bedraggled appearance and dreadfully skinny body. I could see all her ribs, but she had a sweet face and cute ears that stuck straight up in the air.

"What am I going to do with you, then?" Alyson asked her, and received a wag of the tail as a reply.

Alyson had repeatedly said she wouldn't have a second dog to live with us. I think she understood that although I didn't mind other dogs, I have never really wanted to play with them, much less let them into our home. I happily tolerated Valente and didn't mind him coming for walks with us. But if he tried to come into the front garden, I would utter a low, quiet growl of disapproval.

We set off, and the pup trotted along beside us. I knew Alyson wouldn't abandon her. She loves animals too much to do that. Dave had popped out with his camera, so he wasn't home. *I wonder what he'll say when he sees her!*

The pup walked alongside me all the way home, and I let her step into the garden without a murmur. I understood this was different. She needed our help. Alyson brought out food and water for the little scrap who devoured everything, knocking the water bowl over in her excitement. I stood in the doorway and watched.

It was at that moment Dave came home, pulling the car onto the drive. He got out, took one look over the wall, and said,

"Uh-oh!"

"It's alright," Alyson said, "I don't want to keep her, but I couldn't leave her. She's starving, and such a sweet little thing."

"Well, what are you going to do? You can't let her inside the house, and she's probably covered in ticks and fleas."

Our neighbour, Luis, walked past with his dog, and Alyson jokingly said to him, "Would you like another dog?"

"No thanks," he replied, laughing. "One is enough. You'll have to ring the *canil*."

I had heard about the *canil*. It was a locally funded kennel for stray animals. Alyson knew the English lady, Kerry, who ran the charity. She called her and asked if she could help. She had her on speakerphone so Dave could listen in as well, and I sat quietly, wondering what would happen to the little dog.

"Can you keep her overnight?" Kerry asked.

"Not really," Alyson said. "Kat won't like her in the house, and we can't leave her in the garden. She'll just jump over the low wall."

"Okay, I'll come and get her now."

Alyson described where we lived, and Kerry said she was nearby.

While we waited, Alyson continued to fuss over the poor little rescue, and talked to her, explaining what was going to happen.

"If I were keeping you, I'd call you Amber. But a lovely lady will take you with her instead and find you a new home."

I was glad to hear that. She was a bouncy, energetic pup, and I liked our nice, quiet life at home just the way it was.

A few minutes later, Kerry arrived in a pickup truck with a metal cage in the rear. She loaded Amber into the cage, then secured the catch. Kerry explained she thought Amber was probably a failed hunting-dog. They would have simply released her into the wild, as she was no good to the farmer.

Kerry asked how we had found her, and Alyson explained what had happened.

"I'm a bit of a dog-whisperer. Dogs seem to like and trust me."

"Well, don't make a habit of it!" Kerry replied, laughing as she picked up her things and drove away.

Alyson cleared up the food and water bowls and stood looking down the road. Her eyes misted over as she took a deep breath, then walked indoors.

I knew she had grown fond of the little pup, but she came inside and made a fuss of me, and I tried to reassure her she had done the right thing.

Amazingly, only a few days later, Alyson's phone rang.

"That was Kerry from the kennels," Alyson said to Dave after the call had ended. "You'll never guess what. You remember Amber, the little dog I found?"

"The one you fell in love with and wanted to bring home?"

"Yes, well, a couple from Germany have adopted her already. I can't believe it."

"That was quick. It's great news, though. A happy ending."

Several weeks later, Kerry emailed Alyson a photo of Amber. She showed it to Dave. "Doesn't she look happy? She's lying upside-down on her bed and she's smiling."

Alyson patted me. "You have the same expression on your face sometimes, Missy. Like you can't believe how lucky you are."

How true. I still lay awake at night sometimes, remembering how awful my life was before. That dark, dank barn, with water dripping down the walls and in through the roof. The concrete floor of my kennel, and the farmer beating me with the broom handle. Every switch and swipe of the wood against my back stinging and smarting. The pain as I struggled to clamber to my feet and walk afterwards. And the constant snarling hunger that gnawed inside my belly.

The chilling fear that never left me. And the day the farmer dragged my mother away from me. The sound of the shotgun and the crows swirling overhead, screeching their sinister call, wings flapping. Then the silence.

I believed that escaping would mean the end to my problems, but it was only the start of them. I thought I was hungry before, but I had never experienced such a gnawing emptiness as when I was on the streets. It was as if my stomach had turned inside out. The rumble turned to a growl, then a howl, a relentless hollowness that drained me completely.

There were so many moments when I longed to just drop my head to the floor and give up. But something kept me going, plodding forward, one painful step at a time.

I would always be grateful for the day Ginie stopped her car and beckoned me over to her. The day she rescued me, gave me a fresh start, and hope. And then that magical day Alyson and Dave came along and offered me a home. And more love than I could have ever imagined possible. They gave me a family and a future.

The memories of my pups were always with me, though. Some nights I lay in bed and stared up at the stars and imagined they were up there in the sky, each pup a star twinkling and shining down on me. I dreamt that one day I'd be up there with them.

I hoped Alyson and Dave knew how much I loved them. Would always love them. And that, somehow, they'd know one day I'd be a star shining down on them, too.

I snuggled on the bed beside Alyson and sighed. She reached over and caressed me with long, sweeping strokes along my back. Her touch was tender and full of love as I turned around and licked her hand. *Thank you for loving me.*

I curled up, closed my eyes, and fell asleep.

AUTHOR'S NOTE

I n truth, we know nothing about Kat's life before Ginie spotted her walking along the road in the middle of nowhere, somewhere north of Seville. The photographs Ginie took of her were heartbreaking. Kat was mere skin and bone, weighing only eleven kilogrammes, with her matted, bedraggled fur full of ticks and fleas.

We know from her first few weeks with us that so many things petrified her. Her own reflection in the glass from the oven door made her shrink, and even a hand lifted in the air was enough to make her cower. The sight of the *vassoura* broom, traditionally used to sweep houses, made her tremble and roll over in complete submission. The permanent welt marks on the side of her legs and back are testament to the beatings she must have endured.

The vet that sterilised her confirmed she'd had several litters of pups, and from the scar tissue and damage it was obvious they were difficult births. The milk she produced from her teats when Ginie fed her proved she had recently given birth again. Given her emaciated state, the vet agreed those pups would not have survived or even been born full term.

Her fear of birds flying overhead, dark spaces and drains only highlighted the terrors she must have faced in her young life. And yet, despite all those things, there was something in the photograph Ginie posted on Facebook of her latest rescue that captured my heart.

The groomer had recently shaved Kat, removing all her fur and its resident insect population, leaving her almost naked. Nevertheless, she held her head high, showing a quiet dignity and a wisdom in her eyes that belied her years and the horrors she had faced. If the eyes are the windows to your soul, Kat displayed her very nature to me in those milk chocolate coated amber glowing orbs.

I fell in love the moment I met her. The quiet, timid girl that walked slowly up to me, then gazed up into my eyes. My heart was beating so loudly I feared everyone in the room would hear it, as I bent down to stroke her head. Leaving her behind at the rescue centre that morning was an agony like no other I had ever experienced. I wanted to rush back and hold her in my arms and take her home with me there and then. But we needed to plan and set things up ready for her.

The day we collected Kat and brought her home was a magical moment in my life. After waiting and longing for a dog for so many years, I couldn't believe it was finally happening. I knew I would never be the same again as my heart swelled and filled with a love I had never experienced before. I have never wanted children of my own, always joked I didn't have a maternal bone in my body, and yet there I was, totally besotted with my new 'baby'.

I quickly discovered she was an incredibly special dog. I know everyone thinks they have the most wonderful dog in the world, and I'm sure that is true on one level. But Kat was such a wise old soul from the very first day we brought her home. She filled a hole in my heart I didn't even realise was there. Our beautiful little girl that loves routine, adores mashed up sardines on her dinner and long tummy rubs, walks beside the river, rabbits and chickens and sleeping upside down.

So forgive me for the parts of this story that are pure conjecture and fiction. Interwoven with her life with us, and her own stories, are the thoughts that rushed onto the page and refused to be watered down. I've always believed I could see inside the soul of our curly-haired, adorable monkey and imagine what she was thinking. The books I read where the author portrayed an animal as simple and unintelligent just didn't seem to resonate with the girl that can say so much without needing human words.

I hope you enjoyed her story. The rescue dog with the tiny, cropped tail and big heart that has transformed our lives as much as we have transformed hers. Our darling Kat the Dog.

15% of all profits made from the sale of this book will be donated to local dog rescue charities.

YOUR REVIEW

Thank you for buying this book. I hope you have enjoyed reading Kat's story. If you have a moment, I would be delighted if you could leave a review online where you purchased this book. Even a single sentence or brief comment would be lovely. As an indie author, I read and learn something from every remark that is posted, and rely on reviews and recommendations to support and promote my work to a wider audience.

Thank you.

KEEPING IN TOUCH

If you would like to be notified when I publish future books, please contact me via email and I will add you to my mailing list.

author@alysonsheldrake.com

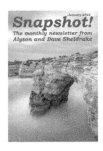   

I also write a monthly newsletter with my husband Dave, which is full of art, photography, book reviews, author interviews, and articles. You can sign up to this free via the link here:

www.alysonsheldrake.com/news/

FREE PHOTO ALBUM

To view the photo album which accompanies this book, please visit my website:

www.alysonsheldrake.com/kat-the-dog

ACKNOWLEDGEMENTS

I am forever indebted to Ginie de Weerd, President of the SOS Algarve Animals charity here in the Algarve. If she hadn't stopped her car that day to help a bedraggled mound of fur walking along the road, we would never have met our darling girl. Kat the Dog has literally changed our lives and we will always be grateful to Ginie for her actions. There are so many charities doing wonderful work in animal rescue. If this book has encouraged even one person to adopt rather than buy their next pet, then it will have done its job.

My wonderful team of beta readers helped to shape this book, giving me wise editorial advice alongside a detailed level of proof-reading and valuable feedback. Beth Haslam, Lisa Rose Wright, Julie Haigh, Val Poore and Liza Grantham––my sincere and heartfelt thanks.

Hats off to the fabulous team of creative talent at MiblArt for designing the cover of this book. They took my ideas and transformed them into the perfect representation of what this story is all about. And they did all that in the midst of the war in Ukraine, where they are based. You guys rock!

Thank you to the wonderful members of the Facebook Group We Love Memoirs. I have made new friends and read so many wonderful books through this group and continue to be amazed at this supportive and encouraging online community of readers and authors.

My thanks must also go to Victoria and Joe Twead, of Ant Press publishing company, for their skill in formatting and presentation.

As always, thank you to Dave, my talented and supportive husband. I love you.

WE LOVE MEMOIRS

The Facebook group *We Love Memoirs* was founded by Victoria Twead and Alan Parks, two memoir writers who created the opportunity to start a community on social media for both readers and authors to get together. The group now has over 6,000 members and continues to grow.

The group covers a whole range of different memoir themes, from comedy and travelogues, to people who have upped sticks and started a new life abroad. There are inspirational and moving accounts of people overcoming abuse, illness, and adversity, and tales of animals, adventures, and resilience.

There is an enormous selection of books to choose from, and the group's page is full of recommendations, new releases, special offers, quizzes, and prizes. You'll find me hanging out there alongside a host of other authors and readers.

www.facebook.com/groups/welovememoirs

ABOUT THE AUTHOR

Alyson Sheldrake was born in Birmingham in 1968. She has an honours degree in sport and has a PGCE (Secondary) qualification in physical education, English, and drama. She has always loved art and painting, although she found little time for such pleasures, working full time after graduation. She joined the Devon and Cornwall Police in 1992 and served for thirteen years, before leaving and working her way up the education ladder, rapidly reaching the dizzy heights of a Director of Education for the Church of England in Devon in 2008.

Managing over 130 schools in the Devon area was a challenging and demanding role, however, after three years her husband Dave retired from the police, and their long-held dream of living in the sun became a reality.

Alyson handed in her notice, and with her dusty easel and set of acrylic paints packed and ready to move, they started their new adventure living in the beautiful Algarve in Portugal in 2011.

She is now an accomplished and sought-after artist working alongside Dave, who became a professional photographer. Being able to bring their much-loved hobbies and creative interests to life has been a wonderful bonus to their life in the Algarve.

Alyson is the editor of *Portugal Letter* magazine, and a feature writer for the Algarve's *Tomorrow* magazine. She is the author of the award-winning and popular *Algarve Blog*, and has also been a keynote speaker for several years at the annual Live and Invest in Portugal international conference.

She is the author of the *Algarve Dream* series of travel memoirs and the author/curator of the *Travel Stories* series of anthologies.

When she is not painting or writing, she can be found walking Kat the Dog along the riverbank at Aljezur in the Algarve, Portugal.

MORE BOOKS BY THE AUTHOR

The Algarve Dream Series

Living the Dream – in the Algarve, Portugal (2020)

And

Living the Quieter Algarve Dream (2020)

Could you leave everything behind and start a new life in the sun?

Have you ever been on holiday abroad and wondered what it would be like to live there?

Alyson and Dave Sheldrake did. They fell in love with a little fishing village in the Algarve, Portugal, and were determined to realise their dream of living abroad. They bought a house there, ended their jobs, packed up everything they owned and moved to the Algarve to start a new life.

Travel alongside them as they battle with Portuguese bureaucracy, set up their own businesses, adopt a rescue dog and learn to adapt to a slower pace of life.

Part guidebooks, mostly memoir; the *Algarve Dream* series of books are a refreshingly honest and often hilarious account of life abroad.

"It felt like I was sitting outside a local *pastelaria* with a new-found friend, drinking a *galão* and sharing a plateful of warm, freshly baked *pasteis de nata* while she told me her story."

Tom George Carroll, Playwright.

A New Life in the Algarve, Portugal – An anthology of life stories (2021)

Meet a whole range of different people who have also made the Algarve their home. Read about the families that moved to live in the Algarve in the early 1970s, before tourism was even an idea.

Follow the artists, writers, and individuals that have set up amazing charities, innovative magazines, and new companies. Discover the stories behind the owner of an award-winning wine farm, the couple who run a yurt farm, a wedding planner, estate agent, rural retreat owners, therapists, and the Vice-Consul to the British Embassy in Portugal.

Read their stories - and be inspired.

Includes a foreword written by the British Ambassador to Portugal.

"This is a well-crafted collection of tales to satisfy anyone's urge to delve into the lives of others and see what makes them tick."

Lisa Rose Wright, author of the Writing Home series of books about life in Galicia, Spain.

"I congratulate Alyson for assembling these stories, all very different but each in its own way communicating a deep affection for this enchanting place at the westernmost tip of continental Europe and its equally enchanting people."

Chris Sainty, Her Majesty's Ambassador to Portugal.

The Travel Stories Series

A collection of short travel stories from all over the world.

Includes work by New York Times bestselling and award-winning travel memoir authors.

Chasing the Dream – A new life abroad (2021)

20 different stories. One shared dream – the chance to start a new life overseas.

Young lives, families, midlife movers, rash spur-of-the-moment property purchasers, and retirement dreamers are all featured in this book. Read about their adventures and find out what it is really like to move abroad.

"Fabulous stories, brilliantly curated by Alyson, showing the ups, downs, laughs and tribulations of living abroad. Once you open the book, you'll struggle to put it down until you've finished and started to plan your new life abroad."

Kevin J D Kelly, author of the Midlife Misadventures Comedy Travel Memoir series.

Itchy Feet – Tales of travel and adventure (2021)

From the Indonesian jungle, to an epic journey out of Africa, and rafting the Zambezi. Find out what Egypt is like in a heatwave, and hunt down Dracula in Transylvania. Catch a rare glimpse into the lives of the last Pech Indigenous people of La Moskitia, Honduras. Be entertained by a teenager's first glance of foreign soil, and an Australian view of England. Ride a Harley through France and Spain and find out what makes someone a perpetual nomad.

"Itchy feet - we have all had itchy feet these past months. Inspired by these talented, including some new, travel writers, I am raring to go again. How wonderful to have such fine writers building on the legacy of authors who first made travel so irresistible for us."

Neal Atherton, author of the Travels in France Series.

Wish You Were Here – Holiday Memories (2021)

We all have that one holiday that stands out in our minds, that one break or vacation we will never forget. Whether it is a childhood 'bucket and spade' family holiday, the 'once-in-a-lifetime' dream destination, your first trip abroad or the city where you first fell in love, the memories are still there today.

The authors in this anthology bring out their postcards and photo albums and invite you to join them as they reminisce about their travels.

"These stories are so full of incredible details that I felt like I was right there with the writer. There are several places I've added to my "have to see before I die" list. There's something for everyone in this fantastic collection of memories."

Tammy Horvath, author and Amazon Reviewer.

The Travel Stories Collection (2021)

This digital box set contains all three books in The Travel Stories Series and also includes 17 Exclusive Bonus Chapters.

77 chapters - almost 50 different authors - covering locations from Africa to The Zambezi. You can travel the world with this box set from the comfort of your own armchair.

"A wonderful collection of short travel stories from all over the world. It is amazing to read all the splendid memories and the authors really take you on a trip full of adventures."

Kathleen Van Lierop, author of the 'mycrazylifefullwithbooks' blog.

For more information on all of Alyson's books, please visit her website:

www.alysonsheldrake.com

Made in the USA
Las Vegas, NV
05 September 2022

54734090R00156